ROUGH
GUIDES

CW01045284

POCKET ROUGH GUIDE
ISLE OF WIGHT

written and researched by
AIMEE WHITE

SHELLFISH

COCKLES
WHELKS
MUSSELS
PEELED PRAWNS
PRAWNS (SHELL ON)
CRAB STIX
PINKS
JELLIED EELS

The island has always been a popular holiday spot: Queen Victoria's physician recommended Ventnor for its therapeutic climate; the romantic poet Lord Tennyson enjoyed strolling across the downs near Freshwater; and Queen Victoria relocated to Osborne House after Albert died. There were other visits from the likes of Charles Dickens, Julia Margaret Cameron and John Keats, and that's only rounding off the nineteenth century. The places they enjoyed are still frequented by visitors today, highlighting the pull the island has on 'mainlanders' (those visiting from mainland England) and further afield.

Most people are drawn in by the island's beaches, which range from Ryde's on the north coast to Compton Bay on the south coast, with plenty more sprinkled in between. Freshwater Bay and Alum Bay on the west coast share their homes with the Needles, whose famed chalked stacks makes it a must-see on anyone's itinerary.

That said, the Isle of Wight is more than simply a bucket-and-spades destination. There's an abundance of history to take in, and in some parts it feels like not much has changed over the years. You can appreciate this at numerous heritage centres across the island or see it first-hand for yourself at the likes of Yarmouth Castle, Old St Boniface

Freshwater Bay

Church and Bembridge Windmill. Chatting with the islanders (or 'nammets' as they call themselves, an old slang word used to describe a snack to eat when working in the fields) is another way to learn about the island's fascinating history on a local level, from tiger cub walks along Sandown beach to *that* infamous Isle of Wight Festival and countless childhood stories retold at Bonchurch Museum.

Of course, seafood features on many a menu, with offerings of fresh Bembridge crab scrawled across blackboards outside cafés and

When to visit

The Isle of Wight, along with the rest of the south of England, generally sees more hours of sunshine than the rest of the country. The island enjoys a relatively mild climate all year round – Ventnor even has its own microclimate – but the **summer** period (May to September) is generally regarded as the best time to visit, and this is when the island is at its liveliest. The cooler **autumn** months are better for anyone planning any extensive walks or cycles. Don't be put off by visiting in the **winter**, with cheaper accommodation rates and ending crisp walks at crackling-fire pubs. **Spring** allows you to see the best of the island's nature with its spectacular flora and fauna, and you can enjoy most of the perks of the high-season without the crowds.

What's new

In 2019, the Isle of Wight received UNESCO Biosphere Reserve status. This means it is now regarded as one of the best places in the world for managed landscapes, where human impact has not taken anything away from the landscape and wildlife. It is just one of seven places in the UK to bear this internationally renowned status, and undoubtedly will promote itself for further sustainability projects.

various fish caught locally and freshly cooked. You can eat out well on the Isle of Wight, with the majority of places very reasonably priced.

The island has long been associated as one of the best places in Europe for dinosaur discoveries, where Cretaceous-age fossils date as far back as 136 million years ago; head to Compton Bay at low tide and you might spot dinosaur footprints. There are also many informative tours and walks led by experts, so you can suss out your flint from your fossils.

Even if the weather isn't on your side, there are plenty of weather-reliant things to do aside from beaches and walks: there's a zoo, loads of museums, a dinosaur theme park and a steam railway. National Trust and English Heritage sites are well represented across the island – from Osborne House to Newtown Old Town Hall – you should also make time to visit the chocolate-box towns of Brighstone, Yarmouth and Godshill. While many enjoy visiting the Isle of Wight as a day-trip from the mainland, to really give it justice, give yourself a long weekend – or up to a week, preferably – to make the most of this underrated island. We promise you won't regret it.

Yarmouth marina

Where to...

Shop

There are few chain brands on the island, with the majority of shops being independent or family-based. There are weekly markets and delicatessens, small boutiques and a few high-street friendlies. Cowes caters to a large sailing crowd, so you'll find specialist stockists such as Musto, Henri Lloyd, Regatta, while Newport has a few more recognisable high steet names. Ventnor is undergoing something of a quirky revolution with its vinyl record shops, vintage clothing boutiques and retro-culture stores. Some shops sell purely island-made products, which is a great way to showcase how much the island has to offer. Wine, gin, cheese, mustard, passata, garlic… the list goes on.
OUR FAVOURITES: Beachcomber, see page 48. Cavanagh & Baker, see page 61. Reggie's Retro, see page 70.

Eat

Perhaps it goes without saying that the island's main cuisine is seafood-based. From seabass and sole to monkfish and mullet, many restaurants pride themselves on sourcing the local catch and cooking it from fresh. It's well worth feasting on much of the island's own produce, which can be enjoyed as part of a picnic or an item to take away. There aren't many international eateries but there are certainly quite a few Italian and French restaurants that are noteworthy, and there are more vegan- and allergy-tolerant spots cropping up. Otherwise, you can't go wrong with the pub classics, from beer-battered cod to island-steak pies.
OUR FAVOURITES: Gastronomy, see page 33. Ristorante Michelangelo, see page 49. Smoking Lobster, see page 70.

Drink

There are lots of pubs dotted around the island; fisherman-type pubs that make for perfect stops at the end of long, windy walks or to take in the breathtaking coastal- and Solent-views. On the island is Island Roasted Coffee, Goddard's Brewery, Rosemary's Vineyard and the Isle of Wight Distillery; you can visit the majority of these as part of a tour with tastings, otherwise you can purchase their products from various shops or order from coffee shops, pubs and restaurants alike.
OUR FAVOURITES: Caffè Isola, see page 42. Isle of Wight Distillery, see page 51. The Old Fort, see page 55.

Go out

Nightlife will never be what the island is famed for: bars and nightclubs are few, but what they lack here they certainly make up for in abundance with their pubs. This is arguably the best way to get under the surface of Isle of Wight culture, with the island well-renowned for its variety of fantastic live music. This may be where you'll find many of the locals; in fact, some evenings you could stroll along a silent high street until you pass a small cove of a pub where all the noise (and people) are contained.
OUR FAVOURITES: The Anchor, see page 35. The Village Inn, see page 62. The Bugle Coaching Inn, see page 89.

Isle of Wight at a glance

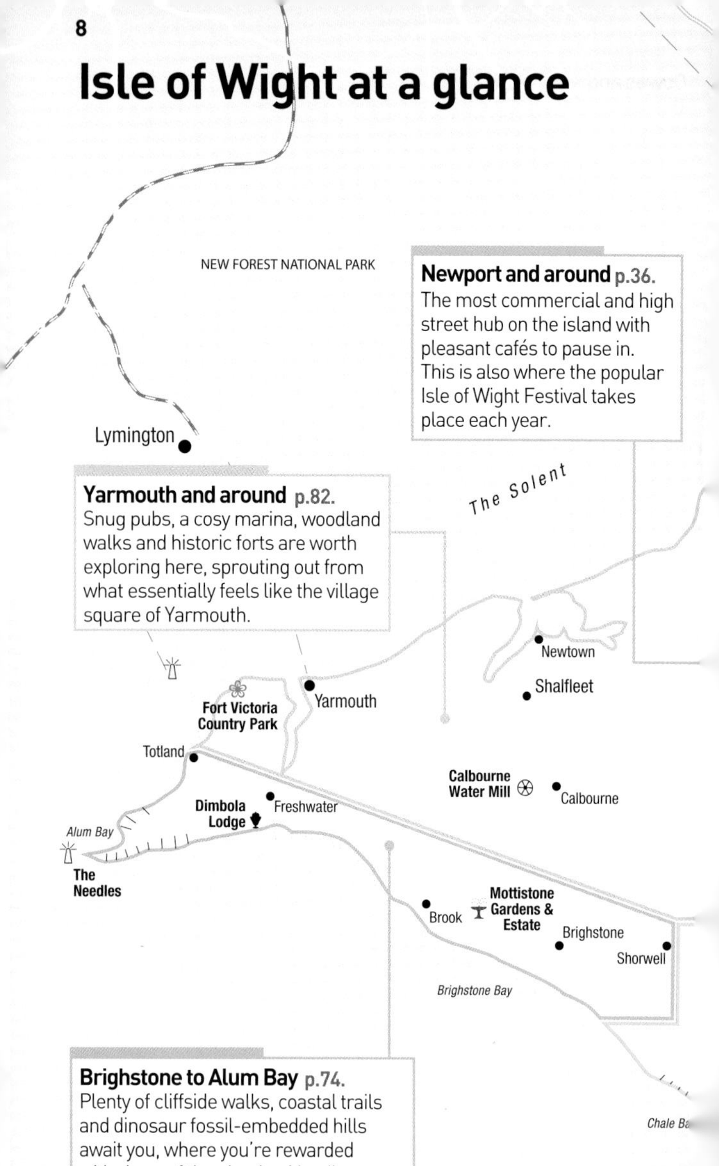

NEW FOREST NATIONAL PARK

Newport and around p.36.
The most commercial and high street hub on the island with pleasant cafés to pause in. This is also where the popular Isle of Wight Festival takes place each year.

Lymington

Yarmouth and around p.82.
Snug pubs, a cosy marina, woodland walks and historic forts are worth exploring here, sprouting out from what essentially feels like the village square of Yarmouth.

The Solent

Newtown

Shalfleet

Fort Victoria
Country Park

Yarmouth

Totland

Calbourne
Water Mill

Calbourne

Dimbola
Lodge

Freshwater

Alum Bay

The
Needles

Mottistone
Gardens &
Estate

Brook

Brighstone

Shorwell

Brighstone Bay

Brighstone to Alum Bay p.74.
Plenty of cliffside walks, coastal trails and dinosaur fossil-embedded hills await you, where you're rewarded with views of the piercing Needles and waves crashing against sandy bays.

Chale Ba

Ventnor to Blackgang p.64.
Vintage tearooms, long-sweeping vistas of the English Channel and an arty, independent edge to enjoy here, all within its own microclimate.

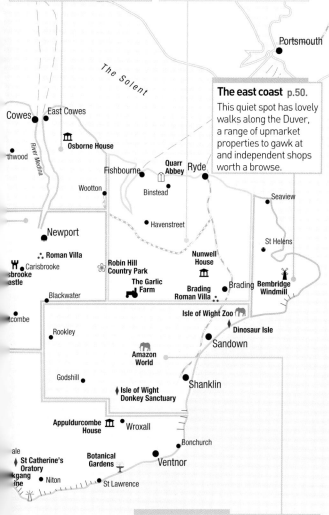

Cowes and around p.26.
This historic yachting town is filled with fashionable boutiques, high-end dining and is the site of the historic Cowes Week and other sailing events.

Ryde and around p.44.
A no-frills seaside stop, perfect for spending days on the beach, filled with fun activities for the kids and splendid views across to Portsmouth on the mainland.

The east coast p.50.
This quiet spot has lovely walks along the Duver, a range of upmarket properties to gawk at and independent shops worth a browse.

The south coast p.56.
Variety of landscapes from the depths of the Chine to the long stretches of beaches, complete with an old-world feel of thatched villages and traditional sweet shops.

The Solent

Portsmouth

Cowes
East Cowes
Osborne House
Fishbourne
Quarr Abbey
Ryde
Wootton
Binstead
Seaview
Havenstreet
St Helens
Newport
Roman Villa
Carisbrooke
sbrooke
astle
Robin Hill Country Park
Nunwell House
Blackwater
The Garlic Farm
Brading Roman Villa
Brading
Bembridge Windmill
tcombe
River Medina
thwood
Rookley
Isle of Wight Zoo
Amazon World
Dinosaur Isle
Sandown
Godshill
Isle of Wight Donkey Sanctuary
Shanklin
Appuldurcombe House
Wroxall
Bonchurch
ale
St Catherine's Oratory
Botanical Gardens
Ventnor
kgang
ine
Niton
St Lawrence

ENGLISH CHANNEL

15

Things not to miss

It's not possible to see everything the Isle of Wight has to offer in one trip – and we don't suggest you try. What follows is a selective taste of the island's highlights, from quaint pubs and intriguing, historic architecture to family-fun activities and bracing, windswept walks.

> The Garlic Farm

See page 39

Spend a morning learning all about garlic (yes, really) by going on a farm tour, before rewarding yourself with a scoop of garlic ice cream afterwards.

< Osborne House

See page 29

Queen Victoria and Prince Albert's family home, an Italianate Renaissance-style villa that makes for a fun day out.

∨ Robin Hill Country Park

See page 40

Tackle a treetop trail, wiggle down a toboggan ride and be wowed at the falconry displays in the 88 acres of woods here.

< **Bonchurch**
See page 66
Delightful village of thatched cottages and Victorian villas, once popular with many Victorian literary icons including Dickens and Keats.

∨ **The Needles**
See page 78
Take the chairlift down from the clifftop over Alum Bay to take in the island's iconic landmark in all its brilliant-white glory.

< **Brading Roman Villa**
See page 52
This impressive villa features incredible mosaics set in a modern museum, where you can learn all about British Roman life during the fourth century.

∨ **Blackgang Chine**
See page 69
Old-fashioned theme park perched on the clifftop; better suited for younger-years, but love it or hate it, it's an island rite of passage.

∧ **Tennyson Down**
See page 78
Beautiful stretch of rolling downs that can be enjoyed as part of a long or shorter walk, and pause by the Tennyson Monument at the top.

< **Isle of Wight Distillery**
See page 51
Sip a Mermaid Gin and tonic while listening to an informal talk about the island's own gin distillery at this laidback pub-bar.

∧ Shanklin Old Village
See page 59
Pink-washed pubs, low thatched cottages, homely pubs with Old English charm... there's no denying that Shanklin is one of the quaintest spots on the island.

∨ St Catherine's Point
See page 68
With its standout lighthouse and medieval tower, there's plenty of maritime history to take in here, with guided tours available.

∧ **The Anchor**
See page 35
Head to this premier live music spot on the island on a Wednesday, Friday or Saturday night for a fun evening of fab jazz, rock or blues.

< **Steam Railway**
See page 41
All aboard this heritage railway, which rolls through five miles of picturesque countryside from Smallbrook Junction in Ryde to Wootton Common.

< **Yarmouth Castle**
See page 83
Once the island's main port, the castle was King Henry VIII's last coastal defence and today boasts superb views over the estuary.

∨ **Coastal walks**
See page 22
There are plenty of coastal trails to enjoy at any time of the year, that wrap around various parts of the island with unique vistas.

Day one on the Isle of Wight

Floating Bridge. See page 26. Take the minute-long chain ferry (or floating bridge) from West to East Cowes, which saves you an 11-mile round trip by road.

Osborne House. See page 29. Spend the best part of the morning exploring the grounds here, which include landscaped gardens, family rooms, a private beach and the smaller Swiss Cottage.

Osbourne House

Lunch. See page 42. Take the bus outside Osborne House to Newport, and stop for a baguette and a slice of cake at *The Blue Door*. Afterwards, wander around the town and check out the likes of the Museum of Island History and the Roman Villa.

Carisbrooke Castle. See page 38. This Norman keep now houses a museum, Edwardian-style gardens and sixteenth-century well-house, as well as resident donkeys. Now an English Heritage site, this is arguably one of the best things to check out on the Isle of Wight.

The Garlic Farm. See page 39. Venture a little outside of Newport, if just to pause for a breather at the popular on-site café at The Garlic Farm. You can even take a guided tour of the site and buy products from their shop, too.

Carisbrooke Castle

Dinner. See page 33. Sample one of Cowes' best restaurants at *Gastronomy*, with their small sharing plates (halloumi fries, calamari) or larger mains (steaks, mushroom courgetti).

Real ale. See page 35. Take a post-dinner stroll along to *The Vectis Tavern*, *Pier Vue* or *The Anchor* for a nightcap, and befriend the locals, yachties or families enjoying a drink (and sometimes live music) there.

The Garlic Farm

Day two on the Isle of Wight

Yarmouth Pier. See page 83. Start the day with a walk along the Victorian, Grade II-listed pier; keep an eye out for shy porpoises at the head or wave at the next ferry entering or leaving harbour. Afterwards, head back to the square to pack for a picnic at the nearby deli, or stop off at the *Gossips Café*.

The Needles. See page 78. Hike along the cliff tops to marvel at the three chalk stacks that once connected the island to the mainland. You can take the chairlift down to Alum Bay to see them down on ground level, or get really up close and personal on a boat tour that zips around them.

Old & New Battery. See page 78. Continue round to take in Victorian coastal defence fort, underground rooms and original cannon guns.

Lunch. Tuck into island-sourced grub on one of the picnic tables or spread out a blanket on the grass.

Tennyson Down. See page 78. Follow the trail along to Freshwater Bay, a route the poet frequently took and became a familiar sight in his long, black cloak. Breathe in the fresh air and stay clear of the cattle.

Dimbola Lodge. See page 76. Take a respite in the tearoom before wandering through the rooms showcasing Victorian Julia Margaret Cameron's photography and equipment used. There's also other exhibitions on display, including iconic photographs and memorabilia from the Isle of Wight festivals.

Dinner. See page 89. *The Bugle Coaching Inn* serves pub grub in a stylish setting. If the weather's nice, enjoy a sundowner outside on the terrace.

Yarmouth Pier

The Needles

Dimbola Lodge

Family island

The island is a perfect destination for families and large groups, and there's plenty of self-catering accommodation; below is a range of recommended activities and sights.

Ryde. See page 44. Kids can frolic on the beach, go wild at the funfair or even go tree-climbing. There's plenty of beachfront eating spots to wind down (or get through) the day with.

Blackgang Chine. See page 69. Entertaining theme park set in a great clifftop spot; it's easy enough to spend a solid day here, and most of the rides are suited for under-12s. Don't miss the daily performances, either.

West Wight Alpacas. See page 85. Spend the day visiting alpacas, llamas, rabbits and more at this farm near Yarmouth, where kids can feed the lambs and everyone can take a llama for a walk.

Ryde seafront

Isle of Wight Zoo. See page 57. Watch the keepers feed the animals, listen to an informative talk and check out the well-cared for Big Cats, monkeys and reptiles.

Dinosaur Isle. See page 59. Learn all about the island's fascinating dinosaur history with life-sized replicas and informative displays, and get hands on with a guided fossil walk – who knows what you might discover?

Isle of Wight Zoo

Robin Hill Country Park. See page 40. Loads of themed play areas that are well-suited to various age groups; activities include zip wires, a maze and falconry displays.

Sandown. See page 56. With its award-winning beach, this traditional resort is a perfect place for kids to lap up the golden sands, fun-filled pier and other seafront attractions. It's one of the best places for holidaying families to base themselves with plenty of family-friendly accommodation around.

Dinosaur Isle

Budget island

Swap fine-dining for picnics and fancy hotels for campsites. It's easy enough to make the most of the island without splashing the cash!

Heritage Centres. See page 64. There are heritage centres dotted all over the island. As they are free to visit and largely reliant on volunteers, you might want to make a small donation, rather than pay an entrance fee. They're a great way to learn about the local history with displays, photographs and other items.

Donkey Sanctuary. See page 67. With over a hundred donkeys and ponies, this sanctuary provides great care for the animals – and it's free, although donations are always welcomed and there are opportunities to adopt a donkey.

Donkey Sanctuary

Rosemary Vineyard. See page 45. See the winemaking process, take a guided tour (30mins) and stroll around the vines, all free of charge. Although the drinks and food served at their coffee shop can be rather tempting...

Coastal walks. Enjoy routes from Colwell to Totland (see page 75), Ryde to Seaview (see page 50) or along Ventnor Esplanade (see page 67). Just lace up a pair of trainers and head out for superlative views. Round it off with a cone of chips or an ice cream on the beach.

Rosemary Vineyard

Picnics. Do your bit for the local community and stock up on local produce for when you're halfway across the headlands and there's not a café in sight. Take your pick from the bakeries, delis and local produce shops.

Steam Railway. See page 41. A full-day unlimited ticket sees you explore the pretty countryside, themed train stations and get half-price entry to the Bird of Prey Centre.

Coastal walk

Walking the island

The Isle of Wight is one of the most popular destinations for walkers across the country, with well-signposted coastal routes providing amazing views in almost every direction.

Cowes to Yarmouth: Start your route in West Cowes along Medina Road; after Thorness Bay you'll wind slightly further inland to Locksgreen and Shalfleet before returning to the coast at Hamsted. The trail leads onto Yarmouth, where this route ends. This is a 16-mile (26km) gentle route with slight inclines.

Yarmouth to Brighstone: This route winds you past The Needles, the island's most iconic sight, in all its ridged-chalk glory. Once you turn the corner, the English Channel will swing into view – you're now on the south of the island – before finishing up at Brighstone Village. This is a 14-mile (23km) route with steep sections.

Sandown to Ryde: This route takes in the buckets-and-spade favourites on the island, starting at Sandown Pier, around to Bembridge Harbour and up through plush Seaview before Portsmouth on the mainland swings into view and it's straight on to Ryde. This is a 12-mile (19km) route that is a fairly gentle route.

Ryde to East Cowes: This historic walk sees you take in abbey ruins, Osbourne House and, if you want to extend your walk, the Royal Yacht Squadron in West Cowes. Starting at lively Ryde, you'll travel a little inland to cross over Wootton Bridge, before passing by Whippingham – near Osborne House – and then coming up to East Cowes, where you can take the floating bridge across to West Cowes. You can continue your walk from here. This is a 8-mile (13km) route that is an easy route with gentle slopes.

Coastal path near Compton Bay

Woodland path near Sandown

Cowes Floating Bridge

Rainy day island

You don't have to time your visit with the summer months. Covering castles to museums and theatres in between, here's how to make the best of a rainy day on the island.

Osborne House. See page 29. While away the best part of a morning exploring the spectacular interiors of Queen Victoria's family home, which include the Indian-decorated Durbar Room, exotic hothouses, nursery rooms and royal bathrooms.

Time for tea. From spacious coffee shops to twee tearooms, there are plenty of places worth stopping off at for afternoon tea, a slice of cake or island-roasted coffee. Get your caffeine fix at Newport's *Caffe Isola* (see page 42) or don your best floral print at Shanklin's *Old Thatch Tearoom* (see page 62).

Shanklin Theatre. See page 59. Year-round productions are held in this Victorian-age theatre, just back from the high street and a 10min walk from the Old Village. There's something for everyone here, from tribute acts and comedy shows to opera performances, and history talks with the likes of Lucy Worsley and wilderness tales with Ben Fogle.

Brighstone Museum. See page 75. Get to grips with life in nineteenth century Isle of Wight – from schooldays to employment – with a visit to this small museum, housed in a traditional rural cottage owned by the National Trust.

Brading Roman Villa. See page 52. This award-winning museum provides a detailed insight into life in Roman Britain; check out the mosaic floors, well-preserved archeology and designated craft areas, breathing life into a time long-gone.

The Durbar Room at Osborne House

Shanklin Theatre

Brading Roman Villa

PLACES

Beautiful coastline

Cowes and around

Cowes sits at the northern tip of the island and is the first port of call for many visitors. This little town is bisected by the River Medina, with lively West Cowes easily accessible to sleepy East Cowes by a floating chain bridge. West Cowes is a haven for yachties, with sailing, boat building and maritime crafts embedded in its history: in 1826, the first Cowes Week commenced here and today it's one of the busiest times of the calendar year. It's also of the most well-heeled areas on the island, its narrow streets filled with boutique shops, old pubs and smart restaurants. That said, East Cowes is home to a smattering of restaurants and Osborne House – which was Queen Victoria's holiday home and later permanent residence – and is perhaps the most popular tourist attraction on the entire island.

The Sir Max Aitken Museum

MAP 30
83 High St, PO31 7AJ. ⓘ 01983 293800, ⓦ sirmaxaitkenmuseum.org. May–Sept Tues–Sat 10am–4pm. Free.
Named after a keen yachtsman who (successfully) represented Great Britain at sailing events, a visit to the small **Sir Max Aitken Museum** is a decent way to learn about the town's maritime history. Set along the high street in an eighteenth-century sailmaker's loft, the museum contains a whole host of maritime paraphernalia: model

The Sir Max Aitken Museum

Classic Boat Museum

boats, figureheads, artefacts from royal yachts and more.

Cowes Maritime Museum

MAP P.30

Beckford Road. ☎ 01983 823433. Mon, Tues & Fri 10am–5pm, Sat 10am–4.30pm; usually closed for one hour between 12.30–1.30pm.
Situated in one large room at the back of Cowes Library, the little **Cowes Maritime Museum** charts the town's sailing and boatbuilding history with a selection of interesting marine and sailing photography, as well as sailing objects and boatbuilding plans. There's also a dress-up box and colouring table for the kids.

Classic Boat Museum

MAP P.30

Albany Rd, PO32 6AA. ☎ 01983 290006, ⓦ classicboatmuseum.org. Tues, Wed, Fri & Sat 10am–4pm, Thurs 10am–1pm. £5 each, combined ticket £8.
The **Classic Boat Museum** is set across two sites: the **Gallery** in East Cowes and the **Boat Shed** in West Cowes. The Boat Shed has over 70 different boats on display, including Sir Ben Ainslie's 2017 America's Cup test boat, while the Gallery

displays more boating memorabilia, which includes various photography series. There's an abundance of items on display here, with informative boards about significant figures in the boating world, from Joe Carstairs, an eccentric 1920s powerboat racer memorialised as 'the fastest woman on water' to local girl Dame Ellen MacArthur, who broke the world record for the fastest solo circumnavigation of the world in 2005.

The Parade

MAP P.30

One of the island's many coastal walks, the route along the **Parade** to Egypt Point features a couple of noteworthy historic points. Starting on Victoria Esplanade at the RNLI Lifeboat Station, you'll pass the Royal Yacht Squadron on your left, once one of Henry VIII's castles and now home to perhaps the most prestigious sailing club in the world, used as a starting point for many sailing races today. This curves onto Queen's Parade, along a short shingle beach and past an otherwise unassuming white cottage, Rosetta Cottage. The plaque on the pavement opposite explains that this was where Lord Randolph Churchill first met and proposed to a Jennie Jerome in 1873; their first son was born in 1874. His name? Winston Churchill. The vista-filled walk ends a little further up at Egypt Point.

Northwood Park

MAP P.28
Northwood House & Park, Ward Avenue, PO31 8AZ. ☎ 01983 293641, ⓦ www.northwoodhouse.org. Free.
The 20-acre **Northwood Park** is a perfect spot for walks, picnics or even a game of tennis or bowls (courts are free to use). The House holds private functions, so you can't go inside, but you can still enjoy the neoclassical exterior, with its palladium front and columns. There are lots of different types of trees here, the majority planted before the nineteenth century, including one supposedly gifted

from Queen Victoria herself. Its position on the hill lends itself to some fine clear sea views.

East Cowes Heritage Centre

MAP P.30
8 Clarence Road, PO32 6EP. ☎ 01983 280310, ⓦ www.isleofwightsociety.org.uk/heritage.aspx. Feb–Dec Mon–Sat 10am–1pm, Wed until 4pm. Free, donations appreciated
Essentially a floor shop that's been converted into a display room, the **Heritage Centre** displays permanent exhibitions of East Cowes' history since 1783. There's an in-depth display about Queen Victoria's fondness of the area – particularly Norris House, where she summered when she was younger (and was the inspiration for Osborne House). It's worth a visit if just to get a background on Osborne House, before you take the trek (or bus) uphill afterwards.

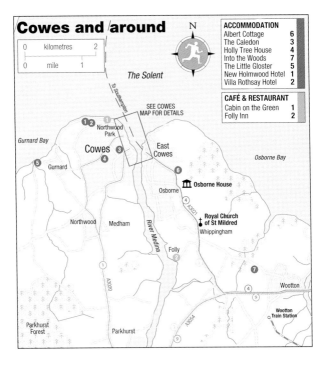

Gardens at Osborne House

Osborne House

MAP P.28

York Ave, PO32 6JX. ☏ 01983 200022, ⓦ www.english-heritage.org.uk/visit/places/Osborne. Daily: April–Sept 10am–6pm; Oct 10am–5pm. May–Oct £18.50, under-16s £11.10; Nov–April £13, under-16s £7.80; EH. Bus #4 to Ryde or #5 to Newport from East Cowes

Here's a little known fact: the young, pre-Queen Victoria used to spend her summers at nearby Norris Castle, but later on, the owner would not sell it to Albert. Undeterred, Albert built **Osborne House** with the help of Thomas Cubitt in the late 1840s, and it became the royal family's holiday home. Styled as an Italianate villa with honey-coloured balconies and expansive terraces, it overlooks sprawling landscaped gardens and on towards the Solent. Today, it's an English Heritage site that should be a must-see if you're in Cowes, or if you have limited time on the island. Although this was Queen Victoria's holiday home, the staterooms are still quite formal, but the private apartments retain a homely feel. Following Albert's death in 1861, Queen Victoria moved into Osborne House until her own death in 1901. The house hasn't really changed too much since then, so this is a fantastic

Cowes Week

One of the oldest and largest sailing regattas in the world, **Cowes Week** (ⓦ cowesweek.co.uk) dates back to 1826, when seven humble yachts took part in a day-long racing event. Fast forward to the present day, up to 1000 boats participate in this world-renowned eight-day regatta, held at the end of July/beginning of August. A range of boats enter various races, whose participants include dedicated hobby sailors, Olympians and world-class yachtspeople. Its bustling, carnival-like atmosphere spills into the streets and transforms the town as it plays host to roughly 100,000 visitors during the week.

All of this does come at a price, though – accommodation prices hike up to **almost double** what you'd usually expect to pay.

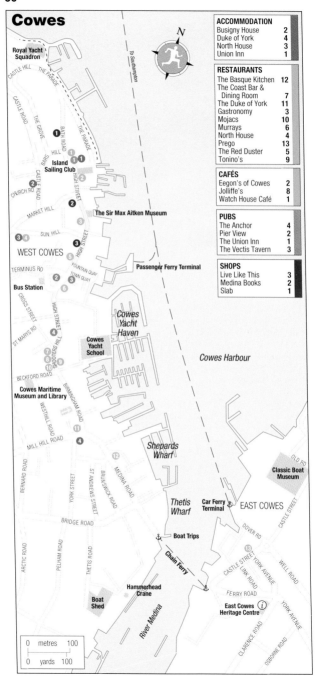

Cowes

To Southampton

N

ACCOMMODATION

Busigny House	2
Duke of York	4
North House	3
Union Inn	1

RESTAURANTS

The Basque Kitchen	12
The Coast Bar & Dining Room	7
The Duke of York	11
Gastronomy	3
Mojacs	10
Murrays	6
North House	4
Prego	13
The Red Duster	5
Tonino's	9

CAFÉS

Eegon's of Cowes	2
Jolliffe's	8
Watch House Café	1

PUBS

The Anchor	4
Pier View	2
The Union Inn	1
The Vectis Tavern	3

SHOPS

Live Like This	3
Medina Books	2
Slab	1

Royal Yacht Squadron

CASTLE HILL
THE PARADE
CASTLE ROAD
THE GROVE
BATH ROAD
BARS HILL
CASTLE ROAD
CHURCH RD
MARKET HILL
SUN HILL
TERMINUS RD
CROSS STREET
ST MARYS RD
HIGH STREET
SHOOTERS HILL
BECKFORD ROAD
BIRMINGHAM ROAD
WESTHILL ROAD
MILL HILL ROAD
BERNARD ROAD
YORK STREET
ST ANDREWS STREET
BRUNSWICK STREET
MEDINA ROAD
BRIDGE ROAD
ARCTIC ROAD
PELHAM ROAD
THETIS ROAD

Island Sailing Club

The Sir Max Aitken Museum

WEST COWES

Bus Station

Passenger Ferry Terminal

Cowes Yacht Haven

Cowes Yacht School

Cowes Maritime Museum and Library

Cowes Harbour

Shepards Wharf

OLD RD

Classic Boat Museum

Thetis Wharf

Car Ferry Terminal

EAST COWES

CASTLE STREET
DOVER RD
YORK AVENUE
WELL ROAD
LINK ROAD
FERRY ROAD
CLARENCE ROAD
OSBORNE ROAD

Boat Trips

Chain Ferry

Hammerhead Crane

Boat Shed

River Medina

East Cowes Heritage Centre ⓘ

0	metres	100
0	yards	100

The world's largest yacht race

The **Round the Island Race** is a one-day sailing event, that first launched in 1931, and competitors come in from far and wide, from the Channel Islands to the USA. Sailing yachts must circumnavigate the island: commencing at the Royal Yacht Squadron (where else?), the route heads westwards round The Needles and St Catherine's Point, on past Bembridge and then back to Cowes, taking four to five hours in all. To find out more, visit ⓦ www.roundtheisland.org.uk.

way to gain an intimate insight into royal family life. And if you want to penetrate that insight even further, a fifteen-minute walk through the gardens leads onto **Swiss Cottage**, where their children made good use of this two-storey playhouse. Afterwards, head down to the private beach, where you can go for a dip or take a peek at her restored bathing machine, a green-pannelled cart that would be wheeled into the sea for Victoria to change and step into the sea from.

Whippingham
MAP P.28

Whippingham is a small village just a mile south of Osborne House, leading on towards Newport; it was once part of the royal estate. It's one of those classic Isle of Wight villages where not much seems to have changed in the past few centuries: think winding country roads, vast green fields and the Royal Church of St Mildred (see below). With its west side flanking the River Medina, you can either pause at the waterside *Folly Inn* (see page 33) or carry on down to the East Cowes Marina, and mooch along the public footpath while passing by sailing yachts and gleaming speedboats.

Royal Church of St Mildred
MAP P.28
April–Oct Mon–Thurs 10am–4pm. Free. Bus #4 or #5 from Osborne House.
The **Royal Church of St Mildred** is pretty much the only sight in

Whippingham, with its humble height and needlelike spires. This Gothic Revival church was where Queen Victoria frequented, and the German Battenberg family (their anglicized name is Mountbatten) have a chapel here. There's also an on-site coffee shop and gift shop.

Gurnard Bay
MAP P.28

Following on from Egypt Point leads immediately onto Prince's Esplanade, which brings you to the quiet village of Gurnard. The Bay is lined with a row of beach huts looking onto a shingle beach, and is a popular spot to discover insect fossils.

Royal Church of St Mildred

Shops

Live Like This

MAP P.30

42 High St, PO31 7RS. ☎ 01983 299599,
Ⓦ livelikethis.co.uk. Mon–Fri 10am–5pm,
Sat 10am–5.30pm, Sun 11am–4pm.

A pretty boutique on the corner
of the high street, somewhat of
a haven for jewellery, lifestyle
furnishings, children's accessories
and perfect for gifts.

Medina Books

MAP P.30

50 High St, PO31 7RR. ☎ 01983 300044,
Ⓦ www.facebook.com/medinabooksiow.
Daily 10am–4pm.

This small, friendly bookshop
supplies a range of paperback and
hardback books, from island-
related titles (maps, nature,
cookery) and fiction to maritime
history and children's.

Slab

MAP P.30

13 Bath Road, PO31 7QN. ☎ 01983 295400,
Ⓦ slabfudge.co.uk. Tues–Fri 11am–4.30pm,
Sat & Sun 11am–5pm (sometimes later).

The husband-and-wife duo who
run *Slab* create artisan fudge on-site
in a range of flavours, from cherry
and lemon meringue to sea-salted
caramel and chocolate orange
(£3.50 each). Large vegan range
and zero-waste packaging.

Restaurants

The Basque Kitchen

MAP P. 30

Medina Rd, PO31 7HT. ☎ 01983 716164,
Ⓦ thebasquekitchen.co.uk. March–Nov daily.

Close to the floating bridge, *The
Basque Kitchen* serves authentic
cuisine from the Basque region,
as well as a range of gluten-free
options. The local-sourced menu
features tapas (roughly £6 each),
salads and steaks, and there's an
extended specials menu, too.

The Coast Bar & Dining Room

MAP P.30

15 Shooters Hill, West Cowes, PO31 7BG
☎ 01983 298574, Ⓦ thecoastbar.co.uk.

Slab

Daily 9am–midnight.

This island-popular bar-restaurant has a lively, sophisticated vibe. On the menu are Hampshire sirloin (£22) and Gressingham duck breast (£17.50). There's also a decent range of wood-fired pizzas (£10.25–13.50).

The Duke of York

MAP P.30

Mill Hill Rd, PO31 7BT. ☎ 01983 295171, ⓦ dukeofyorkcowes.co.uk. Daily 6.30am–12am.

Also a hotel, *The Duke of York* features a great deal of dishes, from pub classics (pies £12.50) and local sea bass (£17.95) to halloumi burgers (£11.95) and fresh baguettes (roughly £5.50).

Folly Inn

MAP P.28

Folly Lane, Whippingham, PO32 6NB. ☎ 01983 297171. Mon–Thurs 11am–11pm, Fri & Sat 11am–midnight, Sun 11am–10.30pm.

Set in the sleepy village of Whippingham, this waterside pub is a perfect stop-off after visiting Osborne House. While you tuck into decent grub (pies, fajitas and more in the £11–£16 range), the river licks the decks. They also run The Folly Waterbus (☎ 07974 864627), a taxi service from Cowes to the nearby jetty.

Gastronomy

MAP P.30

46 High Street, PO31 7BE. ☎ 01983 200666, ⓦ www.gastronomycowes.co.uk. Summer Tues 6pm–late, Wed–Sun noon–late; winter Tues 6pm–late, Wed–Sat noon–late, Sun noon–3pm.

Slick interior and fine meals to match, with the likes of Isle of Wight lamb loin (£18.50) and Malaysian coconut laksa (£11) on the menu. Or pop in for a cocktail – you'll wonder why the place isn't packed all the time.

Mojacs

MAP P.30

10a Shooters Hill, PO31 7BG ☎ 01983

Local ale

281118, ⓦ mojacs.co.uk. Tues–Thurs 5.45–9pm, Fri & Sat until 9.30pm.

Long-serving popular restaurant serving up well-presented dishes at admirable prices, such as grilled bass in Cajun spices (£18) and veg and lentil casserole (£14.50). They also have an extensive gin, wine and cocktail menu.

Murrays

MAP P.30

106 High St, PO31 7AT. ☎ 01983 296233, ⓦ murrays.co. Mon–Sat noon–2.30pm & 7–9.30pm (Fri & Sat until 10pm); Jan closed Mon.

Much-loved seafood restaurant close to the marina, particularly popular with yachting parties. They source local fish so the menu changes depending on the season, or you can opt for a set-price menu (two-course lunch £18, dinner £22) or the catch of the day.

North House

MAP P.30

Sun Hill, PO31 7HY. ☎ 01983 209453, ⓦ northhousecowes.co.uk. Daily: noon–3pm & 6–10pm.

The *North House* offers a fine-dining experience, with a dimly lit ambience apt for couples and

Tonino's

small groups. Starters include six langoustines on ice (£12.50) while mains like the Goan seafood curry (£19) includes clams, crevettes, king prawns and mussels. There's also a separate bar to enjoy an aperitif or digestif by a crackling fireplace. It also functions as a hotel – see our Accommodation chapter.

Prego

MAP P.30

28 Castle St, PO31 6RD. ☎ 01983 293737, ⓦ pregoiow.uk. Mon–Thurs 10.30am–9.30pm, Fri & Sat 10.30am–10pm, Sun noon–8pm.

Informal Italian restaurant-café serving brunch, lunch and dinner right by the Red Funnell port. Busy with locals and visitors alike, enjoy the generous sharing boards (£12.50) or smoked haddock and crayfish risotto (£13.50).

The Red Duster

MAP P.30

37 High St, PO31 7RS. ☎ 01983 290311, ⓦ theredduster.com. Daily 6pm–10pm, lunch only Thurs–Sun noon–2pm.

With a distinctive red exterior and six or so booths inside, there's a jovial atmosphere amongst staff and patrons alike here. Opt for yellowfish sole with asparagus (£16.95) or pork belly with cranberry dauphinoise (£17.50).

Tonino's

MAP P.30

8–9 Shooters Hill, PO31 7BE. ☎ 01983 298464, ⓦ www.toninoscowes.co.uk. Tues–Sat 10am–1pm & 6–10pm.

An inviting ambience and delicious *spaghetti con gamberoni* (£15.95) await you at this long-running family-run Italian restaurant; the extensive menu of authentic pasta, pizza, *pesce* and *carne* dishes will make choosing difficult.

Cafés

Cabin on the Green

MAP P.28

Queen's Rd, PO31 8AU. ☎ 01983 299891, ⓦ www.facebook.com/CabinOnThe GreenCowes.

Small hut on the green that's great for a stop-off for a coffee or ice-cream. Ideally located next to a small patch of green looking towards the mainland including, perhaps slightly less idyllically, Fawley Power Station.

Eegon's of Cowes

MAP P.30

72 High St, PO31 7RE. ☎ 01983 291815,
ⓦ eegonsofcowes.weebly.com. Daily
8am–2pm.

The best breakfast spot in Cowes,
serving Full Englishs' (£6.50),
veggie breakfasts (£7) and plenty
of varieties on toast (from £4.50);
servings are great value for money.
As the sign outside reads, it's
perfect for hangovers.

Jolliffe's

MAP P.30

11 Shooters Hill, PO31 7BE. ☎ 01983
303003. Daily 8.30am–4pm.

Green-tiled Art Nouveau building
serving hearty breakfasts, lunches,
cream teas and hot drinks, with
upstairs seating. The shoe theme
nods to the building's origins as a
bootmaking business.

Watch House Café

MAP P.30

31 Bath Rd, West Cowes, PO31 7RH
☎ 01983 293093, ⓦ watchhousebarn.
co.uk. Daily: May–Oct 8.30am–6pm; Nov–
April 9am–4pm.

At the top of the little road that
leads on down to the RNLI station,
this dinky café serves all-day
breakfasts, homemade cakes and
there's even a small hotel upstairs.

Pubs

The Anchor

MAP P.30

1–3 High St, PO31 7SA. ☎ 01983 292823,
ⓦ www.theanchorcowes.co.uk. Mon, Tues
& Thurs 11am–11pm, Weds, Fri & Sat (live
music nights) until late.

The go-to spot for the island's best
live music, with local and mainland
bands covering all genres, from
rock and jazz to indie and ska.
There's a small 'dancefloor' space
too. There's a choice of real ale,
ciders, beers and wine, as well as
standard pub grub, which you can
enjoy in the beer garden or hunker
down by the fire.

Pier View

MAP P.30

25 High St, PO31 7RY. ☎ 01983 299891,
ⓦ pierviewcowes.co.uk. Mon–Fri
11am–11pm, Sat & Sun 9am–11pm.

This pub and kitchen is popular
with yachties and is good for its
proximity to the ferry terminal.
Although it's primarily a sports
bar, they do serve a decent range
of meals and offer Roast dinners
on a sharing board. There's a nice
selection of beers and wines, too.

The Union Inn

MAP P.30

Watch House Lane, PO31 7QH. ☎ 01983
532444, ⓦ www.unioninncowes.co.uk.
Mon–Fri 7.30am–11pm, Sat 8am–11pm,
Sun 8am–10.30pm.

Low-ceilinged pub hidden down
a snug lane, complete with a log
fire, old maritime paintings and a
slightly tired interior. Food-wise,
choose between the likes of gourmet
burgers or pies (£11), and sample a
range of real ales, spirits or wine.

The Vectis Tavern

MAP P.30

103 High St, PO31 7AT. ☎ 01983 298439,
ⓦ www.vectistavern.co.uk. Mon–Sat noon–
late (usually 2am), Sun noon–midnight.

Established in 1757, this pub is still
just as popular with the locals and
retains real character. It has a beer
garden and hosts quiz nights, live
music and karaoke.

Watch House Café

Newport and around

Newport sits at the centre of the island and is its capital. Although its town centre is pretty generic, Watchbell Lane is a quaint little slice wedged in between the high street shops. Newport is best-known as the site of the Isle of Wight Festival (held at Seaclose Park). Yet venture slightly further out and you'll stumble across some of the island's top attractions, including Carisbrooke Castle, a Roman villa, Robin Hill Country Park and the start of the steam railway. And seeing as many bus routes pass through Newport or require you to transfer buses here, you may as well see what the market town has in store for you.

Museum of Island History

MAP P.38
High St, PO30 1TY. Tues & Thurs 10am–1pm. £1.

Designed by the renowned Regency/Georgian architect John Nash (of Buckingham Palace fame), the Guildhall previously served as a market, fire station and shop – and a banqueting hall that once attracted Prince Albert and other prominent figures. Today it has a slightly more humble position as the island's tourist

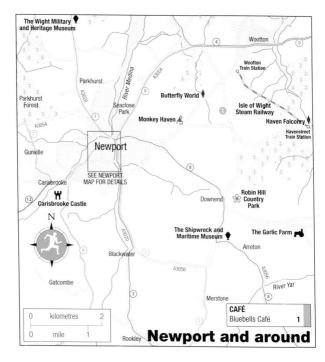

Newport and around

CAFÉ	
Bluebells Café	1

Monkey Haven

office and the **Museum of Island History**. If you're fascinated by dinosaurs or simply want to find out more about the island's enthralling history with them, take in the array of fossils and dinosaur bones that have been collected from the island.

Dinosaurs aside, you can find out much more about the island's history with the likes of photographs, touch-screen displays and even Anglo-Saxon jewellery, swords and axes.

Monkey Haven

MAP P.36
Staplers Road, PO30 2NB. ☎ 01983 530885, ⓦ monkeyhaven.org. Daily 10am–3pm. £10.95, under 15s £8.95 (free 7-day return). Bus #9 to Staplers Road bus stop.

The award-winning **Monkey Haven** is a primate rescue centre housing various monkeys as well as owls, tortoises, meerkats and reptiles (including Teddy, a retired bearded dragon). There are keeper talks throughout the day and opportunities to get up close with the animals, and there's also a café on site.

Newport Roman Villa

MAP P.38
Cypress Rd, PO30 1HA. ☎ 01983 529720, ⓦ iwight.com/Visitors/Where-to-go/Newport-Roman-Villa. April, May, June & Sept Mon–Sat 10.30am–3.30pm; July & August daily 10.30am–4pm. Adults £3.75, under 17s £2.75. 10min walk from town centre.

If you take the signposted walk (roughly 10mins) just south of Newport you'll come across the remains of a **Roman villa**. The remains are believed to be that of a farmhouse dating back to 280 AD; you can see the hypocaust underground heating systems that the Romans were ingenious with, along with reconstructed sections of the villa that the farmhouse belonged to. It's a gentle introduction to Roman life on the Isle of Wight; but the Brading Roman Villa (see page 52) fills in more of the gaps.

Carisbrooke Castle

Carisbrooke Castle

MAP P.36

Castle Hill, PO30 1XY. ☎ 01983 522107,
🌐 https://www.english-heritage.org.
uk/visit/places/carisbrooke-castle.
Feb half-term daily 10am–4pm; March
Wed–Sun 10am–4pm; April–Sept daily
10am–6pm; Oct daily 10am–5pm; Nov to
mid-Feb Sat & Sun 10am–4pm. Adults
£10.50, under 17s £6.30; EH. Bus #6, 7,
12 or 38 pass nearby

Southwest of Newport lies one of
the Isle of Wight's most prominent
attractions, **Carisbrooke Castle**.
This Norman keep hilltop fortress's
main claim to fame was being the
place where Charles I was confined
prior to his execution in London.
There is a **museum** at the castle's
centre and an Edwardian-style
Princess Beatrice Garden, named
after Queen Victoria's youngest
daughter. Overloaded with history?
Greet the donkeys at the sixteenth-
century well-house, before strolling
along the battlements to marvel at

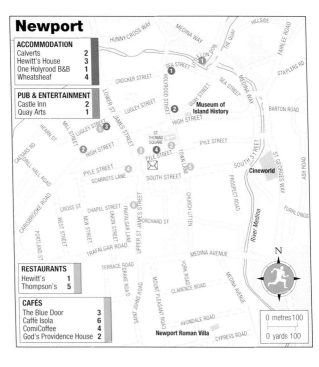

International Classic Car Show

The **International Classic Car Show** kicks off at Newport Quay, where hundreds of classic cars – vintage, classic, custom, rare and retro – descend from all over the UK and Europe. This two-day event, usually held in September, has been running since the early 1990s, with the Saturday in Newport and the Sunday in Ryde. It is free to attend, and it's a charity event, so all funds raised go towards local charities.

the views (for once, not of the sea) across inland Isle of Wight.

The Shipwreck and Maritime Museum

MAP P.36

Arreton Barns Craft Village, Main Rd, PO30 3AA. ☎ 01983 533079, ⓦ shipwreckcentre. com. April–Oct daily 10am–4.30pm. £5, under 15s £2.50. Bus #8 from Newport or Sandown.

The Shipwreck and Maritime Musem is made up of three galleries and intriguing displays of artefacts rescued from various wrecks around the island. Highlights include 'seabed scenes', an eighteenth-century diving barrel and items recovered from a tragic shipwreck during the First World War. It's four miles south

of Newport, and leads on nicely to the Arreton Down Nature Reserve.

The Garlic Farm

MAP P.36

Mersley Lane, Newchurch, PO36 0NR. ☎ 01983 867333, ⓦ thegarlicfarm.co.uk. Daily 9am–5pm. Free.

Is **The Garlic Farm** one of the quirkiest things to do on the Isle of Wight? We like to think so. Around four miles southeast of Newport, learn about all things garlic, or more popularly take a Garlic Farm tour by foot or tractor. If you want to take some of the good stuff back home with you, there's plenty to choose from: garlic ice cream, garlic mayonnaise and even black garlic vodka. It's also a popular spot for food, with

The Garlic Farm

The Isle of Wight Festival

The first **Isle of Wight Festival** was held in 1968, not far from Godshill. Around 10,000 attended the one-day event that saw the likes of T-Rex, Jefferson Airplane and The Pretty Things perform, with tickets priced at £1.25. The 1969 festival moved to Wootton with 150,000 attendees flocking to see the likes of Bob Dylan, The Who and more; but it was the 1970 spectacle that truly rocked the boat. 600,000 (some say 700,000) festival-goers descended to East Afton Farm to get their hippy on to Joni Mitchell, John Sebastian, The Doors and The Jimi Hendrix Experience. However, such scenes (think naked-bathing hippies en-masse) caused a local uproar and the "Isle of Wight Act" was implemented, which prevented any unlicensed gatherings of over 5000 people. It took 32 years before the island dared/was allowed to host another such event; in 2002, the festival was revived in Newport. This second-coming Isle of Wight festival is now a musical mainstay.

its restaurant and café serving garlic-infused dishes (no surprises there). There's no such thing as too much garlic as far as the farm is concerned – which is probably why their annual garlic festival is so popular (August; ⓦ garlic-festival.co.uk). Look out for their products on sale and ingredients on menus around the island.

Isle of Wight Steam Railway

Robin Hill Country Park

MAP P.36

Downend, PO30 2NU. ⓣ 01983 527352, ⓦ robin-hill.com. March Sat–Thurs 10am–5pm; Easter to early Sept daily 10am–5/6pm; Oct half-term daily 10am–10pm. Peak £23, off-peak £17.50, under 4s free; tickets valid for seven days unlimited visits. Bus #8 from Newport to Sandown.

Set in 88 acres of woodland, **Robin Hill Country Park** is pure family fun. Why not traipse along the treetop trail or catch one of the amazing daily falconry displays? Whether you want to get up high with ziplining or stay on ground-level with the woodland pond or Chinese Temple, the expansive site accommodates for varying age groups. All aboard the Cows Express train ride, breeze along the Canopy Skywalk and try not to get lost in the wooden maze. And, if you decide to swing by in October, you'll catch the light display performances – just visit the website for more details.

Robin Hill Country Park

Isle of Wight Steam Railway

MAP P.36

Havenstreet, PO33 4DS. ☏ 01983 882204, Ⓦ iwsteamrailway.co.uk. March–Oct daily plus special services in Dec. Full-day unlimited ticket £15 (£13 online), under 17s £7 (£6 online). Bus #9 from Newport. The **Isle of Wight Steam Railway** sets off from Wootton Common through rolling countryside to Smallbrook Junction, and is a fab way to feel like you've travelled back in time and take in the picturesque views. The trains are all renovated steam engines, many retired from previous service on the island, with some dating as far back as the nineteenth century.

The main station is at Havenstreet, where more fun for all ages awaits. There's a play area, a museum and a viewing gallery, where you can watch goings on in the railway workshops. Ticket-holders also get half-price entrance to the **Bird of Prey Centre** (Ⓦ haven-falconry.co.uk).

The Wight Military and Heritage Museum

MAP P.36

490 Newport Rd, PO31 8QU. ☏ 01983 632039, Ⓦ wmahm.org.uk. Mon–Sat 10am–4pm (last entry 3pm). Take bus #1, #51 or #52 to County Showground.

The **museum** offers guided tours from ex-service volunteers. There's a range of tanks, vehicles (including a French ambulance), uniforms and interesting artefacts dating from the nineteenth century onwards, as well as a replicated typical street scene – think red brick walls and Union Jack bunting. There's also an air rifle range and on-site tearoom, *Churchills*. You also have the opportunity to take a ride on one of the vehicles on Tuesdays, Thursdays and Saturdays.

Butterfly World

MAP P. 36

Staplers Rd, PO31 4RW. ☏ 01983 883430, Ⓦ butterflyworldiow.com. Mon–Sat 9.30am–4pm, Sun 10am–4pm. Proudly promoting itself as the 'fifth butterfly farm in the world', **Butterfly World** makes for a great rainy-day option. Look out for the different types of butterflies settling on the plants and leaves around you, where you can also get to grips with their life cycle. Aside from the butterflies there are ornate Japanese and Italian gardens, and you can also feed the fish in the Koi ponds.

God's Providence House

Restaurants

Hewitt's

MAP P.38

33 Lugley St, PO30 5ET. ☎ 01983 822994,
ⓦ hewittshouse.com.restaurant. Tues
6.30pm–10pm, Wed–Sat noon–1.30pm &
6.30–10pm, Sun noon–2.30pm.

Stylish restaurant with a relaxed
atmosphere. Their contemporary
British cuisine is well-presented
with the likes of bacon-wrapped
chicken breast (£16) and grilled
seabass fillets with triple-cooked
chunky chips (£17), all served with
a side of veg. They also have a small
hotel above.

Thompson's

MAP P.38

11 Town Lane, PO30 1JU. ☎ 01983 526118,
ⓦ robertthompson.co.uk. Wed–Sat
noon–2.30pm & 5.30–9.30pm.

Michelin-starred is on the menu,
thanks to chef Robert Thompson.
Thompson's has a cosy bar, open
kitchen and more tables upstairs,
and it's easy to see why this spot
is a popular choice. The menu
changes with the seasons, but with
the two-course set menu (£29,
three courses £35) you can expect
dishes such as haddock croquette
and slow-cooked venison – or you
can push the boat out with the £79
eight-course tasting menu.

Cafés

Bluebells Café

MAP P.36

Briddlesford Lodge Farm, Wootton, PO33
4RY, 3 miles east of Newport ☎ 01983
882885, ⓦ briddlesford.co.uk/bluebells.
Daily 9am–5pm; also some Sat evenings
from 6.30pm.

This is a great café to come to for
island-produced food (sandwiches,
hot mains), some of which comes
from their own farm. Try to nab
a table in the chic little courtyard,
mooch around the on-site farm
shop (perfect for picnics or gifts)
and say hello to the animals in the
cowsheds. The family-run farm
opened their café (once the cattle's
winter housing) in 2009. Visit their
website for details of live music
nights – their resident band is the
aptly named The Herd.

The Blue Door

MAP P.38

18 St James' Square, PO30 1UX.
ⓦ facebook.com/www.thebluedoorcafe.
Mon–Sat 9am–4pm.

Pleasant café on the corner of the
high street serving homemade
breakfasts, lunches and cakes
(baguettes from £4.25). Somewhat
unexpectedly, their speciality is
"Bunny Chow", a South African
dish consisting of curry served in a
loaf of bread (from £8.25).

Caffè Isola

MAP P.38

85a St James St, PO30 1LG. ☎ 01983
524800 ⓦ islandroasted.co.uk. Mon–Sat
7.30am–6pm, Sun 9am–5pm.

Spacious coffee shop spanning
two floors where you can order
breakfast, lunch and drinks from
on the ground floor and browse a
selection of local products upstairs.
They roast their own coffee, Island
Roasted, which can be found
across the island. They also have
a small roastery machine upstairs.
Whether you're passionate about
coffee or simply want some space,

this is the best place in Newport to find it.

ComiCoffee

MAP P.38
59 Pyle St, PO30 1UL. ☎ 01983 559000
Ⓦ comicoffee.uk. Mon–Sat 8am–6pm, Sun 9am–4pm.

This coffee house-cum-comic store is a relaxed place to hang out, read comics or browse memorabilia for sale. Choose between waffles (caramel apple £7.50) or paninis (mozzarella, tomato and pesto £5.50) with a selection of teas, coffees and speciality milkshakes. They also host evening events, like comic book artist sessions.

God's Providence House

MAP P.38
85a St James St, PO30 1SL. ☎ 01983 522085 Ⓦ godsprovidencehouse.com. Mon–Sat 9am–5pm, Sun 10am–3pm.

Housed in one of the oldest buildings in Newport, this teahouse epitomises Old-English charm with twee furnishings and touches. As is expected, they do a cracking afternoon tea for two (£24.95), breakfasts (from £4.25) and light lunches (brie and red pepper quiche £5.75), as well as Sunday roasts.

Pub

Castle Inn

MAP P.38
91 High St, PO30 1BQ ☎ 01983 552258, Ⓦ thecastleinniow.co.uk. Mon–Thurs & Sun 11am–11pm, Sat & Sun until 1am.

The *Castle Inn* is Newport's oldest pub, dating all the way back to 1550 and the last in England to be granted a cock-fighting licence in 1705. This old-brick building serves real ales and ciders and dishes sourced from local suppliers, with live music at the weekends. It's also believed to be haunted by the ghosts of a young man, woman and cat…

Entertainment

Quay Arts

15 Sea St, PO30 5BD ☎ 01983 822490, Ⓦ quayarts.org. Craft shop and café Mon–Sat 9am–5pm, café also Sun 10am–4pm.

This arts centre is housed in three converted warehouses which overlooks the harbour. Inside, there are various exhibitions, concerts, film and comedy, while outside you can pause for food or a drink on the café's chilled-out terrace.

Quay Arts

Ryde and around

Nestled between Cowes and Bembridge, Ryde lies on the north-east of the island. This is where the Hovercraft service runs between Portsmouth, just a short hop across the waves. There are wide-stretching views of the glittering mainland from sandy Appley Beach, which principally makes it a seaside resort (and a lot of fun at that). Once a popular Victorian holiday resort, with a shopping arcade to boot, there are still some faded Art Deco hotels and other rundown buildings that are slightly stuck in the recent past – but with a belt of beachfront restaurants, child-friendly pub gardens and enough sand for everyone, it's a perfect spot either for a day-trip or as a starting (or ending) point for your trip around the Isle of Wight.

Ryde pier

MAP P.46

Ryde's nineteenth-century **pier** is a major transport hub, with a train station at each end and ferries mooring against it. While you can drive or walk along to the pier's end, there's not much to do aside from picking out the details of Portsmouth just ahead on the mainland – but if you've just arrived from there, what's the point? There's much more fun to be had under the pier, instead. Weather permitting, you can explore the long sandflats under the pier at low tide and be amazed at the marine wildlife – it's unlike anywhere else on the island, thanks to rich anemone fields and sponge gardens. There's an annual Under the Pier event which is great fun for

Appley Tower and beach

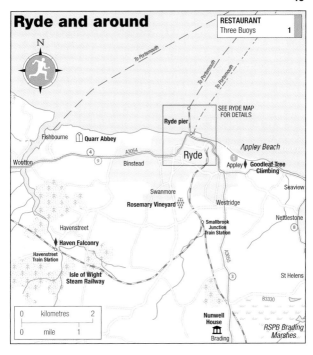

Ryde and around

RESTAURANT
Three Buoys   1

families and reveals a fascinating scene for biologists alike.

Appley Beach

MAP P.45

Lying to the east, where the sands back onto the leafy parkland of **Appley Park**, **Appley Tower** is a stone folly built in 1875, now open as a shop-museum filled with fossils and gemstones. It's a nice stretch of beach looking across the Solent to the striking Spinnaker Tower.

Goodleaf Tree Climbing

MAP P.45

Appley Lane/Park, PO33 1ND. ☎ 0333 800 1188, ⓦ goodleaf.co.uk. £33/climber, discounts for 3+ groups; 5 percent discount if you walk or take public transport there. April–Oct 9.30am–2.30pm & 5–7pm; Nov–March email ✉ info@goodleaf.co.uk to check availability.

Tucked away in Appley Park, just behind the beach, **Goodleaf Tree Climbing** is a great way to pass a

sunny morning. The climbing takes place up a magnificent 70ft oak tree, set amid a green space of ancient woodland that used to be part of a manor house. Once you're dangling from the canopy, you'll have a unique panoramic of the Solent and island coastline. It's a little tricky to find – there's no building or site centre – but is accessible by walking along the Esplanade, or through the park. Check the website for a detailed route on how to get there.

Rosemary Vineyard

MAP P.45

Smallbrook Lane PO33 4BE, ☎ 01983 811084, ⓦ www.rosemaryvineyard.co.uk. April–Sept Mon–Sat 10am–5pm, Sun 10am–4pm; Oct Mon–Sat 10am–5pm, Sun 10am–4pm; Nov–March Mon–Sat 10am–4pm, Sun 10am–4pm; closed Sun in Jan and Feb. Free; free guided winery tours Sat–Tues 11am, 12pm & 1pm.

One of the largest producers of English wine, the wines, liqueurs and ciders are made onsite at

Rosemary Vineyard. Visitors can see the winemaking process, stroll around the vines, watch a short film, or take a guided winery tour which includes tastings. There's an onsite coffee shop, *The Vineleaf*, serving wine and freshly ground coffee, light lunches and homemade sweet treats.

The Isle of Wight Bus Museum

MAP P.46
Park Road, PO33 2BE. ☎ 01983 567796, ⓦ iwbusmuseum.org.uk. April–Oct Wed, Thurs & Sun 10am–4pm. Free; souvenir guides £4.50.

The appealing **Isle of Wight Bus Museum** has a colourful collection of over 20 historic buses that once plied the island, including an 1890's horse-drawn stagecoach, and pictures, paintings and artefacts of various forms of transport over the years. Check the website for details of the Rydabus Running Day, usually in May, when some of the buses that can still work leave their garage for a day out. Also worth checking out is the Classic Buses, Beer and Walks Weekend (see page 118), where 100 vintage buses cover a series of routes serving participating island pubs – a whole lotta fun.

Donald McGill Postcard Museum

MAP P.46
Royal Victoria Arcade, Union St, PO33 2LQ. ☎ 01983 717435, ⓦ saucyseaside postcards.com. Mon–Sat 11am–4pm. £3.

Nestled away in the depths of the Royal Victoria Arcade, the **Donald McGill Postcard Museum** is jam-packed with smutty postcards (the clue is in its website name) created by artist Donald McGill. The cartooned cards, which reached the height of their popularity in the 1930s, featured a simple scene with a comical caption – for example, a gentleman inspecting a busty

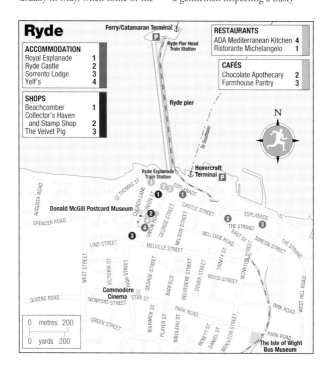

Quarr Abbey

woman's necklace with the line "I think they're wonderful!" and the like. Many were traditional seaside scenes, which Ryde has long been a popular spot for, and some of the postcards were even banned for indecency until as late as the 1960s.

Quarr Abbey

MAP P.45
Just outside the village of Binstead, near Ryde, PO33 4ES. ☏ 01983 882420, Ⓦ quarrabbey.org. Mon–Sat 10am–4/5pm, Sun 11.15am–4/5pm. Free. Buses #4 & #3 stop outside the abbey.

Two miles west of Ryde, outside the village of Binstead, is one of the island's earliest Christian relics, **Quarr Abbey**. Founded in 1132, the abbey was named after the quarries nearby, where stone was mined for use in the construction of Winchester and Chichester cathedrals. You can wander freely around the beautiful grounds – there's an orchard, a woodland walk and pigs and chickens to admire – plus you'll find a very fine teashop with outdoor tables and a farm shop selling produce from the island and the abbey itself, including ale, cider and honey.

International scooter rally

A rather peculiar event ocurrs every August Bank Holiday (the last weekend in August), when up to 5000 scooters descend onto Ryde for the world-renowned **Isle of Wight International Scooter Rally**. Since 1980, decked-out Vespas, Lambrettas and other scooters – think furry leopard print seats, colourful artwork, dozens of front-lights – and their riders take to the streets of Ryde and Sandown, in what is estimated as the largest single gathering of scooters in the world.

Watch the procession as they make their way across the island and enjoy evening entertainment with nights like Best of British, '60s Soul and Best of Mod. Their rally base is in Ryde so this is the best place keep your eyes out for a pack of 'peds streaming past.

Shops

Beachcomber

MAP P.46

3 Union St, PO33 2DU. ☎ 01983 568632,
ⓦ www.facebook.com/Beachcomber-
1185853008206500. Mon–Sat 10am–5pm.
Delightful coastal-themed
shop selling painted driftwood,
nautical trinkets and other quirky
furnishings, all of which make
for thoughtful gifts and unique
homeware.

Collector's Haven and Stamp Shop

MAP P.46

Royal Victoria Arcade, PO33 2LQ. Daily
9am–5pm.
Inside the crumbling Royal
Victoria Arcade, this shop is filled
with a variety of collectables,
including vintage glass bottles,
beermats, matchboxes, cigarette
boxes and the like.

The Velvet Pig

MAP P.46

44 Union St, PO33 2FF. ⓦ thevelvetpig.com.
Tues–Sat 10am–5.30pm.
Vintage clothing (shoes, jewellery,
coats, skirts, dresses, shirts) from
all eras. Also sells a range of quirky
enamel pins. It's a real feast for the
eyes: no two pieces – or customers
– the same.

Restaurants

ADA Mediterranean Kitchen

MAP P.46

55 Union St, PO33 2LG. ☎ 01938 564023.
Mon–Sat 11.30am–3pm & 5.30–10pm, Sun
5.30–9pm.
Friendly restaurant serving
Turkish and Mediterranean
dishes, such as *kleftiko* (£16.95),
hot *meze* options at £5.50 (falafel,
whitebait, *borek*) and salmon *tava*
(£17.95).

Collectors Haven Ryde Stamp Shop, Royal Victoria Arcade

Union Street

Ristorante Michelangelo

MAP P.46

81 Union Street, PO33 2DL. ☎ 01983 811966, Ⓦ www.ristorantemichelangelo. co.uk. Daily (except Wed) noon–3pm & 5–10pm.

A local's favourite, serving authentic Italian cuisine alongside a selection of vintage Italian wines. They also have a delicatessen shop and café. Opt for tagliatelle Bolognese (£12.50) or duck with a blackcurrant sauce and veg (£18.50), washed down with a medium-sweet Orvieto Classico Amabile white wine.

Three Buoys

MAP P.45

Appley Lane, PO33 2DU. ☎ 01983 811212, Ⓦ threebuoys.co.uk. Mon–Sat 11.30am–9pm, Sun 11.30am–8pm.

Award-winning restaurant serving lunch, dinner and Sunday roasts on the seafront. The upstairs restaurant has a large balcony overlooking Ryde beach and excellent views of the Solent. Dishes include mussels in a cream and cider sauce (£14.50) and crispy halloumi with harissa yoghurt, tomato salad and *dukkah* (£11.50).

Cafés

Chocolate Apothecary

MAP P.46

7 Esplanade, PO33 2DY ☎ 01938 718292, Ⓦ chocolateapothecary.co.uk. Mon–Sat 10am–5pm, Sun 10am–4pm.

This yummy chocolate shop-café is set in a former Victorian fishmonger's, but thankfully it's just chocolate on the menu today. Just across from the Hovercraft and bus terminals, this spot sells perfectly giftable home-made chocolates, or simply sip a rich hot chocolate in one of their window seats. Bliss!

Farmhouse Pantry

MAP P.46

8 The Esplanade, Ⓦ www.facebook.com/ farmhousepantry. Daily 10am–late.

This 50s American diner is kitted with red leather booths, framed prints of James Dean, Marilyn Monroe and Elvis, and it doubles up as an ice cream parlour in the summer. No-frills breakfasts and lunches (full English breakfast £6.95, Thai curry £9.95, fresh Bembridge crab baguettes from £4.50). Try out their 3-for-£10 seafood tapas (crab fritters, mackerel on toast, calamari and more).

The east coast

The east coast of the Isle of Wight is home to a peppering of little villages like Seaview and Bembridge, and clusters of lesser-visited beaches and walks. Pleasant St Helens is nestled between Seaview and Bembridge and provides amazing views over the bustling Bembridge harbour; the Duver meanwhile makes for a pleasant stroll, flanked with its sandy beach on one side and colourful beach huts and a large café on the other. Away from an abundance of nature and wildlife, you can also find out more about the historical landmarks that line this dreamy eastern coast of the island, from the Brading Roman Villa to the Tudor-Jacobean Nunwell House.

Seaview

MAP P.50

Bus #8 from Ryde

East of Ryde, the first port of call is **Seaview**; during the day it makes for a nice stroll along the seafront promenade from one town to the other, with the Solent on one side and tree-lined fields on the other. This small resort is much less brash and far more genteel; it's a popular spot for politicians who have holiday homes here. While there aren't any beaches here, there are

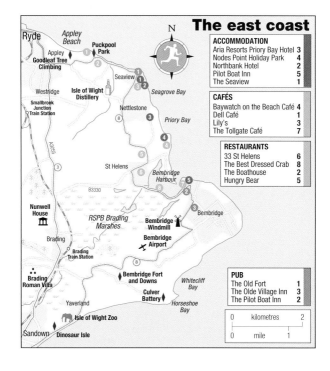

The east coast

ACCOMMODATION

Aria Resorts Priory Bay Hotel	3
Nodes Point Holiday Park	4
Northbank Hotel	2
Pilot Boat Inn	5
The Seaview	1

CAFÉS

Baywatch on the Beach Café	4
Dell Café	1
Lily's	3
The Tollgate Café	7

RESTAURANTS

33 St Helens	6
The Best Dressed Crab	8
The Boathouse	2
Hungry Bear	5

PUB

The Old Fort	1
The Olde Village Inn	3
The Pilot Boat Inn	2

0	kilometres	2
0	mile	1

Seaview

fishermen's cottages and swanky modern houses to gaze at as you pick your way through the narrow roads, otherwise hunker down in one of the cosy pubs or continue down to Seagrove Bay and beyond.

Isle of Wight Distillery

MAP P.50

The Mermaid Bar at the Wishing Well, Pondwell Hill, PO33 1PX. ☏ 01983 613653, ⓦ isleofwightdistillery.com. Summer daily 11am–11pm; Winter Mon–Wed 11am–5pm, Thurs–Sun 11am–11pm. Bus #8 to Wishing Well bus stop.

The **Isle of Wight Distillery** produce Mermaid Gin, Mermaid Pink Gin and HMS Victory Navy Strength Gin, as well as a Mermaid Vodka and HMS Victory Navy Strength Rum. The talks and tastings take place in an informal setting at a gastrobar: order a drink at the bar and enquire when the next talk is, then take your place by the glass window, behind which is the working distillery equipment. They host up to ten talks a day (no crowd is too small) before tastings at the end. There are 10 botanicals in the Mermaid Gin, three of

which are island locals (Boadicea hops, elderflower and rock samphire) and the pink and blue bottles are art pieces in themselves, made from Murano glass in Venice.

Priory Bay

MAP P.50

You can reach **Priory Bay** by walking from Seaview, which will also see you take in Seagrove Bay. Backing onto National Trust-owned woods, this 700m-long sandy strip is one of the best beaches on the island, and as such there's a luxury hotel here with private access to part of the beach, and a holiday park. It's a popular spot for yachties who usually anchor here to wait for the right tide, before continuing down past St Helen's and onto Bembridge.

Bembridge

MAP P.50

Bembridge is a quiet, well-heeled village with an assortment of cafés and restaurants clustered next to the yachtie-filled Bembridge Harbour – the harbour itself bustles with sailing yachts, moored houseboats and eager paddleboarders. Stroll along Embankment Road for views of the bobbing boats with their clanking masts, and continue to St Helen's.

Bembridge Windmill

MAP P.50
High St, Bembridge, PO35 5SQ. ☏ 01983 873945, ⌨ nationaltrust.org.uk/bembridge-windmill. Mid-March to Oct daily 10.30am–5pm. £5.90, children £2.95; NT. Bus #8 from Ryde, Sandown or Newport.

Just north of Bembridge sits **Bembridge Windmill**, a Grade I-listed structure dating back to 1700. Although it looks rather dilapidated now, back in its heyday it ground the flour that was sold to the Navy. This was where the naval ships moored before they steered onwards to the Battle of Trafalgar. Naval battles aside, you can climb to the top of the windmill which lends itself to brilliant views over Culver Down, and you can also find out more about how the windmill once operated.

Brading Roman Villa

MAP P.50
Morton Old Rd, Brading, PO36 0PH. ☏ 01983 406223, ⌨ bradingromanvilla.

org.uk. Daily 10am–4pm. £9.50, under-17s £4.75. Bus #2 or #3 to Yarbridge Cross bus stop, then 10min walk (follow signs).

The modern museum at **Brading Roman Villa** houses the West Range, which was built around 300 AD, while you can see the chalk outlines of the North and South Ranges outside. The well-preserved mosaic of Medusa is believed to have warded off evil, while the Bacchus mosaic was a (welcomed) sign of drinking and entertainment. Kids can dress up as Romans while everyone else can take a break at the café, whose terrace has views overlooking the nearby coast.

Nunwell House

MAP P.50
Brading, PO36 0JQ. ☏ 01983 407240, ⌨ nunwellhouse.co.uk. £8, under 16s £2, garden only £5. Late May to mid-July Mon 1pm–4.30pm; guided tours 1.30pm & 3pm (45min–1hr); hours vary so check website.

Nunwell House is a historical house that's been in the Oglander family since 1522. Its main historical claim to fame was being the place where Charles I spent his last night of freedom before he

Bembridge Windmill

The RNLI

The **Royal National Lifeboat Institution** (RNLI) is a registered charity responsible for providing lifeboat search and rescue services 24 hours a day, all year round. To see a lifeboat speed down the ramp on its way to a 'shout' (callout) is a fantastic sight – perhaps not for the sailors in distress, but certainly for anyone lucky enough to watch it from the safety of shore.

As with the rest of the UK, the RNLI depends entirely on volunteers. Below are the addresses for the lifeboat stations on the island; there are also small gift shops selling RNLI merchandise, with all funds going towards the RNLI.

Bembridge: ⓦ www.bembridgelifeboat.org.uk
Cowes: ⓦ www.cowes-lifeboat.org.uk
Yarmouth: ⓦ www.yarmouthlifeboat.org.uk

went on to become imprisoned at Carisbrooke Castle (see page 38) and then onto London's Whitehall, where he was executed. You can visit the house as part of a guided tour, and there are five acres of gardens to explore at your own leisure, including a nineteenth-century walled garden. Needless to say it's a popular wedding venue, with neo-classical statuary, well-clipped lawns perfect for romantic strolls and large atmospheric rooms.

St Helens

MAP P.50

ⓦ nationaltrust.org.uk/st-helens-duver.
St Helens is a tiny little village – one of the smallest in the country, in fact – and as such, with its rolling green fields, is a popular area for campsites. The Duver, just a short 10min walk from the village, started off as the island's first golf course during the Victorian age. Today, it's a National Trust site, with sandy beaches, coastal woodland walks and cragged rock pools. There's also a variety of wildlife thriving here, which doesn't seem all too surprising, what with its genteel feel of the **Bembridge Lagoons** and surrounding area.

Culver Down and Culver Battery

MAP P.50

Culver Down, also known as **Bembridge Down**, is another popular walking route, with a clifftop trail and its highest point at 104m (341ft). It is also home to a coastal artillery **battery**, used in the First and Second World Wars, to protect against enemy ships attempting to enter the Solent. For many years, it was closed to the public and used as a military zone, but nowadays it is a National Trust-owned sight. While there are a couple of Second World War artefacts still visible on the headland, you can experience a much more peaceful side to the area now, with picnic benches and beautiful, wide-sweeping coastal views to appreciate – and not a warship in sight.

Horseshoe Bay

MAP P.50

Not to be confused with Horseshoe Bay in nearby Bonchurch, this **Horseshoe Bay** lies at the base of the white cliffs of Culver Down, whose familiar shape gives this small spot its name. It's advised to only try to access the beach at low tide, when the largest amount of beach is exposed; you can also access the Bay by boat, but only at high tide. There are also two caves nearby, slightly less-appealingly named The Nostrils.

Restaurants

33 St Helens

MAP P.50

Lower Green Road, PO33 1TS. ☎ 01983 872303, Ⓦ 33-st-helens.co.uk. Lunch Thurs–Sat noon–2pm, Dinner Tues–Sat 6–9pm.

Owned and run by a husband-and-wife duo, *33 St Helens* serves modern European food with immaculate presentation. The menu may change seasonally but it's a popular spot for returning visitors. And with light bites including sea salt and rosemary roasted nuts (£3), mains such as hake fillet with a herb and truffle crust (£20) and salted caramel semifreddo (£8) for dessert, who can blame them?

The Best Dressed Crab

MAP P.50

Fishermans Wharf, Embankment Rd, PO35 5NS. ☎ 01983 874758, Ⓦ thebestdressedcrabintown.co.uk. Daily 10am–late; Jan & Feb Sat & Sun only.

This family-run restaurant has been operating for almost two decades; they specialise in locally caught crab and lobster, as well as local Bembridge prawns (season only). Choose from lobster-, crab- or other seafood-filled sandwiches, salads or seriously salivating platters, with produce also available to buy from their shop. Outdoor seating overlooks the picturesque Bembridge Harbour.

The Boathouse

MAP P.50

Springvale Rd, PO34 5AW. ☎ 01983 810616, Ⓦ theboathouseiow.co.uk. Daily 9am–11pm (food until 9pm).

Less than two miles east of Ryde (also accessible on foot along the coast), this upmarket gastropub has a garden with fantastic views across the Solent. A great spot for a drink, it serves baguettes, Sunday lunch and fancier dishes such as game pie (£14.95) and local pork, apple and black pudding sausages (£12.95). They also offer accommodation.

Hungry Bear

MAP P.50

Fakenham Farm, Eddington Rd, St Helens, PO33 1XS. ☎ 01983 718871, Ⓦ thehungrybear.org.

Two tips when visiting the *Hungry Bear*: book a table, and turn up hungry. Predominately serving huge breakfasts, Sunday Roast platters and double-stacked lamb burgers, you'll want to go on a long walk afterwards – you can take the pleasant walk down to the Duver which makes for a much-needed post-*Bear* stroll.

Cafés

Baywatch on the Beach Café

MAP P.50

The Duver, St Helens, PO33 1YB ☎ 01983 873259, Ⓦ facebook.com/pages/Baywatch-on-the-Beach/1456944517873609. Mon & Tues 9am–5pm, Wed–Sun 9am–9pm.

Average salads, veggie bites and light meals served at this café, but in a fab spot overlooking the Solent that makes it a good place to take a break from the beach, especially if kids are in tow. There's also a picturesque row of colourful beach huts just a little further down the path. Usually open summer only.

Dell Café

MAP P.50

Puckpool Sands, Seaview, PO34 5AR. ☎ 01983 812947, Ⓦ dellcafe.com. Daily 9am–4.30pm.

Set on the sea wall, *Dell Café* has a country farmhouse-style interior with views spanning Puckpool Sands and yachts gliding past on the Solent. They serve an eclectic mix of brunch, lunch and dinner options (potato and chorizo hash £7.75, hanging beef skewer £17.50), and, as is common in most places on the island, dogs are very welcome.

Lily's

MAP P.50

15 High St, Seaview, PO34 5ES. ☎ 01983 617367, Ⓦ www.facebook.com/

LilysCoffeeShop. Mon–Fri 8.30am–5pm, Sat 9am–5pm, Sun 9am–4pm.

There's a cosy feel to this family-run café, using grandma's recipes, milk from Briddlesford Farm and island-roasted coffee. Choose from paninis, wraps and quiches – or try a ploughman's sharing board for two (£12.95) and chill out on one of the sofas.

The Tollgate Café

MAP P.50

Embankment Rd, Bembridge PO35 5NR. ☎ 01983 872742. Daily 10.15am–5pm.

It doesn't look like much from the outside – essentially a no-frills, humble green cabin – but it is a great spot to stop for a coffee and slice of cake, while the kids, dogs or anyone else with too much energy can run around outside in the green space that overlooks the harbour. They also have a selection of books that you can curl up with: needless to say, this place comes highly recommended by locals and visitors alike.

Pubs

The Old Fort

MAP P.50

The Esplanade, Seaview, PO34 5HB. ☎ 01983 612363, ⓦ oldfortbarcafe.co.uk. Tues–Sat 11am–late, Sun 11am–5pm; food

served until slightly earlier.

This slick café-bar retains a fisherman's inn-vibe with its nautical decor (sails, shipping maps, oar rowlocks) and Simon & Garfunkel usually on play. Superb views of the Solent and a perfect place to pause to get the wind out of your ears, while you tuck into classic pub grub.

The Olde Village Inn

MAP P.50

61 High St, Bembridge PO35 5SF. ☎ 01983 872616, ⓦ yeoldevillageinn.co.uk. Mon–Fri noon–midnight, Sat till 1am, Sun till 10.30pm.

Serving real ales from across England, *The Old Village Inn* has supposedly served pints of the good stuff since 1787. There's DJ nights on Fridays, and Saturdays give way to live music nights – a classic slice of island culture.

The Pilot Boat Inn

MAP P.50

Station Rd, Bembridge PO35 5NN. ☎ 01983 872077, ⓦ thepilotboatinn.com. Daily noon–10pm, Fri & Sat till 11pm.

From the outside, the bottom half of *The Pilot Boat Inn* is styled like a ship, complete with portholes. Inside, it is a cosy yet sleek affair, with bar snacks and pub food to feast on. They also run a small B&B, with cycling storage and ferry/hovercraft travel discounts on offer.

The Boathouse

The south coast

The south coast of the Isle of Wight has a great deal on offer. First of all, there's the resort town of Sandown, which suits families well with the likes of the pier, Isle of Wight Zoo and Dinosaur Isle. Further down is Shanklin, a chocolate-box of a village, with dinky thatched cottages and award-winning gardens. They're both popular seaside resorts but while Shanklin retains an old-fashioned charm, Sandown has seen better days, and as such, isn't worth prioritising as much as Shanklin. That being said, there are splendid coastal walks worth taking, especially heading east towards the headland of Whitecliff Point.

Sandown

MAP P.58

Sandown is a traditional seaside resort town that is best-suited for families looking to stay put in one place, although it's not too far from Shanklin at all. Sandown Bay was awarded 'Beach of the Year' in the 2019 BBC Countryfile Magazine Awards; usually lively but now a little faded, Sandown has been a long-time beachside favourite, with a five-mile stretch of beach that's perfect for sandcastle-building, darting to and from the sea and more. The only other real main thing to do here is a venture to the nineteenth-century **pier**.

Sandown Pier

MAP P.58

The Esplanade, PO36 8JT. ☎ 01983 404122, ⓦ sandownpier.co.uk. Arcade daily: April–Sept 9am–11pm; Oct–March 9am–10pm.

Sandown Pier

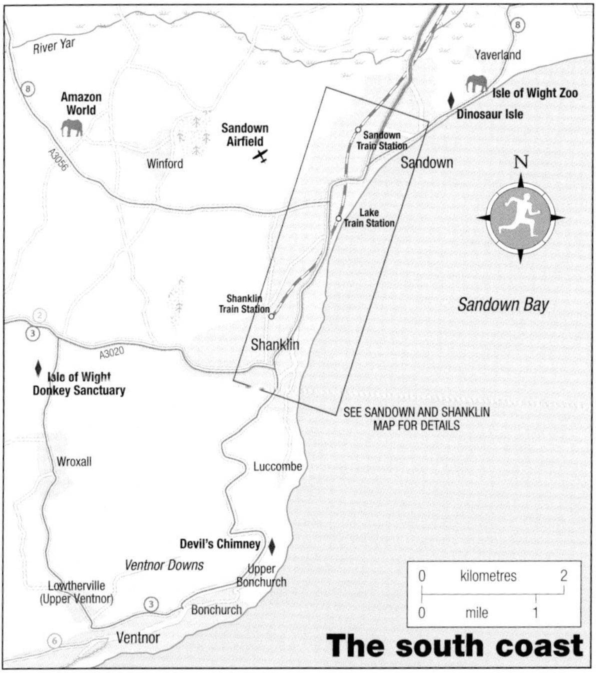
River Yar
Amazon World
Sandown Airfield
Winford
A3056
Yaverland
Isle of Wight Zoo
Dinosaur Isle
Sandown Train Station
Sandown
N
Lake Train Station
Shanklin Train Station
Sandown Bay
Shanklin
A3020
Isle of Wight Donkey Sanctuary
SEE SANDOWN AND SHANKLIN MAP FOR DETAILS
Wroxall
Luccombe
Devil's Chimney
Ventnor Downs
Upper Bonchurch
Lowtherville (Upper Ventnor)
Bonchurch
Ventnor
0 kilometres 2
0 mile 1
The south coast

Pier April–Sept only. Individual charge for attractions; pier free.

The **pier** used to be a popular entertainment hall but is now a garish amusement arcade with crazy golf, bowling and dodgems, and there's also a bar, café and ice cream kiosk. It makes for a good rainy-day option. For a more scenic experience, you can walk out to the pier head, where fishermen try their luck at catching the various species of fish and spider crabs that live beneath the pier.

Isle of Wight Zoo

MAP P.57

Yaverland Road, PO36 8QB. T 01983 403883, W isleofwightzoo.com. Daily: April–Oct 26th 10am–5.30pm, Oct 27th–3rd Nov 10am–5pm, 4th Nov–1st Dec 10am–4.30pm. Adult £12.55, under 14s £10.23. Buses #2, 3, 4 and 24 to Newport/Shanklin.

The **Isle of Wight Zoo** is situated at the far end of the seafront parade, closer to Bembridge than Sandown. The zoo is home to circus-rescued Big Cats, Madagascan lemurs and several species of monkeys, along

Dinosaur Capital of Britain

The Isle of Wight has long been recognised as one of the best European destinations for **dinosaur remains**, with over 20 species of dinosaur having been identified here. In 2019, the fossilised remains of a **giant pterosaur fossil**, known as Hatzegopteryx, were discovered embedded in the cliffs along the southwest. The giant had a wingspan of at least 20 feet and lived around 125 million years ago, with rumours flying that it was the largest species ever to fly during the Late Cretaceous period.

Sandown and Shanklin

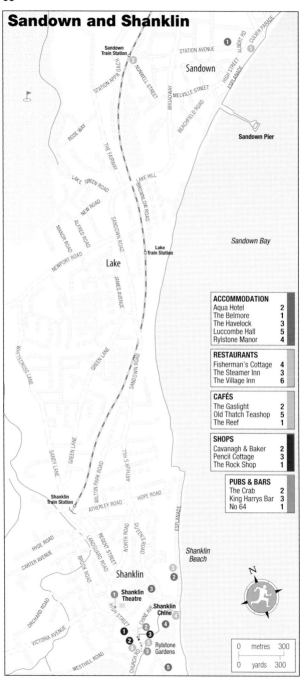

Sandown Train Station

STATION AVENUE

STATION APPROACH

NUNWELL STREET

Sandown

ROSE WAY

THE FAIRWAY

LAKE GREEN ROAD

NEW ROAD

ALFRED ROAD

MANOR ROAD

NEWPORT ROAD

LAKE HILL

BROADWAY

MELVILLE STREET

BEACHFIELD ROAD

HIGH STREET

ALBERT RD

CULVER PARADE

ESPLANADE

Sandown Pier

BROWNLOW ROAD

SANDOWN ROAD

Lake Train Station

Lake

Sandown Bay

JAMES AVENUE

WHITECROSS LANE

GREEN LANE

SANDY LANE

GREEN LANE

SANDOWN ROAD

WILTON PARK ROAD

ARTHUR'S HILL

ATHERLEY ROAD

HOPE ROAD

Shanklin Train Station

ESPLANADE

Shanklin Beach

HYDE ROAD

CARTER AVENUE

LANDGUARD ROAD

BROOK ROAD

REGENT STREET

NORTH ROAD

QUEEN'S ROAD

ORCHARD ROAD

VICTORIA AVENUE

HIGH STREET

Shanklin Theatre

Shanklin

CHINE AVE

Shanklin Chine

CHURCH RD

Rylstone Gardens

WESTHILL ROAD

N

ACCOMMODATION
Aqua Hotel	2
The Belmore	1
The Havelock	3
Luccombe Hall	5
Rylstone Manor	4

RESTAURANTS
Fisherman's Cottage	4
The Steamer Inn	3
The Village Inn	6

CAFÉS
The Gaslight	2
Old Thatch Teashop	5
The Reef	1

SHOPS
Cavanagh & Baker	2
Pencil Cottage	3
The Rock Shop	1

PUBS & BARS
The Crab	2
King Harrys Bar	3
No 64	1

0	metres	300
0	yards	300

Dinosaur Isle

with various reptiles and farm animals. Amazingly, the zoo owners used to walk the tiger cubs along Sandown Beach, back in the 1970s and 1980s. Make sure you squeeze in enough time to listen to one of the informative talks about the animals, and watch the keepers feed them, both of which take place throughout the day.

Dinosaur Isle

MAP P.57

Culver Parade, PO36 8QA. ⓣ 01983 404344, ⓦ dinosaurisle.com. Daily: May–Aug 10am–6pm; Sept, Oct & April 10am–5pm; Nov–March 10am–4pm. £5, children £4.
A little further along from the zoo and towards Sandown Bay is **Dinosaur Isle**. Everyone can learn something here with its expansive fossil collection, interactive displays and replicas of the various species that once roamed (and have been found) on the island – after all, the Isle of Wight is one of the best areas in Europe for dinosaur remains and fossils, so a visit here won't be in vain. They also host guided geology, fossil and landscape walks (bookings essential; separate charges apply).

Shanklin

MAP P.58

Shanklin merges with Sandown, but the two resorts couldn't be more different (aside from the fact they're both extremely family friendly). It's best to tackle Shanklin in three parts: the new town with its high-street shops and theatre; the quaint Old Village at the other end with its thatched cottages and traditional stores; and, down the lift, steps or chine, the beach resort, with huge beachfront pub-restaurants and holes of souvenir shops selling buckets, spades and ice creams. As well as varied nature and geology in its cliffs, beach and chine, you can also enjoy interesting historic walks of the area, or spend the evening at **Shanklin Theatre** (ⓦ www. shanklintheatre.com).

Shanklin Chine

MAP P.58

Chine Hill, PO37 6BW. ⓣ 01983 866432, ⓦ shanklinchine.co.uk. Jan–early Nov daily 10am–7pm. £4.60, under-15s £3.
The pathed stepway twisting down the tree-lined gorge known as **Shanklin Chine** is a natural wonder of beauty. The word

Shanklin beach

'Chine' is only used in the Isle of Wight and the neighbouring mainland town of Dorset, and is an old Saxon word meaning a deep, narrow ravine. With a waterfall at the top and a nature trail to follow down to the bottom, this steep route drops 32m in just over a quarter of a mile, and eventually leads onto the beach. You'll pass by over 150 varieties of wild plants, ferns and mosses along its nature trail, as well as a variety of caged bids, from grey wagtails to Senegal parrots. Aside from its ancient and Victorian heritage, it played its part during World War II, where soldiers trained on the steep slopes. Down on sea level, there's a tearoom and nineteenth-century *Fisherman's Cottage*.

Amazon World

MAP P.57

Four miles northwest of Shanklin at Watery Lane, PO38 0LX. ☎ 01983 867122, ⊕ amazonworld.co.uk. April–Oct daily 10am–5.30pm (last admission 4.30pm); Nov–March opens at 10am but closing time varies: call to check. £12.95, under-15s £10.95. Bus #8 from Sandown.

It's not quite the same level as neighbouring Sandown's Isle of Wight Zoo, but the mammals, birds and reptiles on display at **Amazon World** is an impressive collection, with the likes of armadillos, toucans, sloths and piranha fish – the keeper talks and feeding sessions are worth sticking around for, too. It's on the way to Newport, so a good option if you're looking to begin or tail-end your trip with an animal-friendly stop-off.

Rylstone Gardens

MAP P.58

11 Popham Rd, PO37 6RG. ⊕ www. facebook.com/rylstonegardens. April–Oct 10.30am–4pm.

The award-winning **Rylstone Gardens** is a lovely place to relax, with a humble bandstand, old-fashioned tearoom (cream tea £5.50), crazy golf and craft cabins selling local artwork and accessories. It's a tranquil spot where you can take a breather and there's also an abundance of wildlife to keep your eyes out for, from red squirrels and cute robins to chirping birds and rare butterflies.

All scooters lead to Sandown

While the International Scooter Rally has had their base at Smallbrook Stadium in Ryde since it first started in 1982, in 2019 it was announced that the rally base would be shifting across to Sandown. The new rally base is set to be at Sandown Airport, which will give scooterists the space to enjoy the usual entertainment, as well as a camping area. Taking place at the same time of year (the August Bank Holiday, the last weekend in August), it's thought that the 5000-odd riders that descend to the island will give a much-needed boost to the Sandown area.

Shops

Cavanagh & Baker

MAP P.58
103 High St, PO37 6NS. ☎ 01983 506590,
Ⓦ www.cavanagh-baker.co.uk. Tues–Sun
10am–4pm.

Emporium selling Isle of Wight-made products, from soaps and calendars to seagrass candlesticks and tea towels. Extensive wine and beer collections from the likes of Rosemary Vineyards and Goddards Brewery, and a tasty selection of jars of island chutney, pesto, pickles and passata.

Pencil Cottage

MAP P.58
22 Church Rd, PO37 6NU. Gift shop Mid-March to Oct daily 10am–5pm; Nov & Dec closed Mon & Fri. Tearooms April–Oct daily 10am–5pm.

Seventeenth-century thatched cottage where English romantic poets Keats and Longfellow once bought their pencils from (hence the shop's name). An array of gifts and souvenirs in two small rooms, which leads through to a quaint and very popular tearoom (cream tea £4.95).

The Rock Shop

MAP P.58
91–93 High St, PO37 6NF.

Be warned, this sweet shop will give your eyes toothache – the floors, walls and products are all neon-coloured – and is somewhere Willy Wonka would be proud of. It takes the form of a traditional sweet shop, with huge jars filled with rock sweets, handmade fudges, and other classic sweeties, but there's also some sugar-free options. Aside from sweets, they sell a range of island specialities, including mustard, shortbread and honey. There's also a branch on the high street in Sandown.

Restaurants

Fisherman's Cottage

MAP P.58
Shanklin Esplanade PO37 6BN. ☎ 01983 863882, Ⓦ fishermanscottageshanklin.

Fisherman's Cottage

co.uk. Late March–early Nov 11am–9pm Tues–Sat, until 4pm Sun.

Nestled beneath Shanklin Chine at the furthest end of the esplanade, this thatched dining pub serves lunch, light bites and evening meals. The cottage was built by William Colenutt in 1817, who also created the pathway through the Chine just behind it, and was once visited by a young Queen Victoria.

The Steamer Inn

MAP P.58

18 Esplanade, PO37 6BS. ☎ 01983 862641, ⓦ thesteamer.co.uk. Daily 10am–11pm; food served Mon–Sat 10–11am & noon–9pm, Sun noon–8.30pm.

With panoramic sea views from the veranda and a homely styled interior apt for a fisherman's front room, *The Steamer Inn* offers a varied menu: choose from jacket potatoes (£6.10) and pub favourites to burgers (from £11.35) and hearty fish stews (£12.45). Plenty of veggie and gluten-free options, too.

Old Thatch Teashop

The Village Inn

MAP P.58

1 Church Road, PO37 6NU. ☎ 01983 865500, ⓦ facebook.com/pages/Village-Inn/148572178515106. Sun–Thurs 11am–11pm, Fri & Sat 11am–midnight.

Old English charm, with a darkly lit ambience, plush armchairs, grandfather clocks and a roaring fireplace. Bar at the centre and table service available on both floors; homemade dishes aplenty but their Sunday roasts (turkey £9.95; beef £10.25) are a real feast. Live music on Sundays.

Cafés

The Gaslight

MAP P.58

Sandown Station PO36 9BW. ☎ 07595 670101, ⓦ www.facebook.com/gaslightcafeiow. Mon–Fri 9am–4pm.

This dinky diner-meets-tearoom hosts a range of quirky lunchtime and evening events, including vintage-themed and Northern Soul nights, and live jazz.

Old Thatch Teashop

MAP P.58

4 Church Rd, PO37 6NU. ☎ 01983 865587, ⓦ www.oldthatchteashop.co.uk. March–Oct daily 1am–5pm.

With an icing-pink exterior and very twee interior, this is somewhere Dolores Umbridge from *Harry Potter* would appreciate. The building dates back to 1690 but today you can enjoy various afternoon cream teas (Victorian Tea £9.95, £18.95 for two), jacket potatoes and light bites such as gluten-free asparagus and stilton quiche (£6.50).

The Reef

MAP P.58

Esplanade, PO136 8AE. ☎ 01983 403219, ⓦ thereefsandown.co.uk. Daily 11am–11pm; food served until 9pm.

This small, contemporary-styled café-bar is just a stone's throw from Sandown beach, offering the likes of stone-baked pizzas (from £9.95),

Fish and chips at *The Crab*

or you can simply pop in for a coffee. Either way, you can choose to cosy up indoors or take in the great views of the award-winning Sandown Bay on the decking. There's a surf school next door, too.

Pubs

The Crab

MAP P.58

94 High St, PO37 6NS. ☎ 01983 862363, Ⓦ www.greeneking-pubs.co.uk/pubs/isle-of-wight/crab. Mon–Thurs & Sun 11am–11pm, Fri & Sat 11am–midnight; food served until 10pm (9.30pm on Sun). Thatched pub nestled in the heart of Shanklin's Old Village, serving food at great value. There are daily offers and savers menus, while the main menu features prawn cocktail starters and steak and kidney pie for mains. There's also a beer garden out front.

King Harry's Bar

MAP P.58

6 Church Rd, PO37 6NU. ☎ 01983 863119, Ⓦ www.kingharrysbar.co.uk. Mon–Sat

11am/noon–11pm, Sun noon–10.30pm. Yet another charming thatched building in Shanklin Old Village, with a small selection of real ales on tap and lagers, and a garden that backs onto the Chine walk. Food is served May–Sept only, with each dish named after Henry VIII's wives – Catherine Parr is a rack of lamb (£13.50) while Anne of Cleves is breaded scampi (£9.50).

No 64

MAP P.58

64 High St. ☎ 01983 716460, Ⓦ no64highst.co.uk. Thurs–Sun 5pm–late (Sat from noon).
Cocktail bar serving the classics (most £8) and even a 'mar-tree-ni' of 12 cocktails (the clue is in the name). Other alcohol options are locally sourced: spirit liqueurs, wine, gin and beer all come from the island. They also host cocktail masterclasses, but for those not drinking, you can go for food (paninis, deli boards, afternoon tea and more).

Ventnor to Blackgang

Although each region of the Isle of Wight has its own distinct character, Ventnor feels somewhat removed from the rest of the island – perhaps a little like a Mediterranean-on-sea, with its similar microclimate. It has long been a popular seaside resort, with the neighbouring suburbs of Bonchurch and St Lawrence making pleasant stop-offs. Towering above all three is St Boniface Down, the highest point on the island at 236m (787ft). The Down's minor landslides created the sheltered Undercliff, which gives Ventnor its very own microclimate. With excellent coastal paths, it's a perfect spot for walkers; families will have plenty of fun at Blackgang Chine funfair; and everyone else will rejoice at the charming thatched village of Godshill, one of the best on the island. With its bunting-clad high street filled with independent shops, Ventnor is also arguably the creative heart of the island, and is the home of the annual Ventnor Fringe Festival.

Ventnor Beach

MAP P.66

A walk along the Esplanade takes you past the fishing harbour, a small strip of restaurants and

shops such as the island-favourite *Smoking Lobster*. The **beach** is a rich red with never-ending views across the English Channel: in fact, you are closer to Cherbourg in France than you are London.

Botanical Gardens

Ventnor Heritage Centre

MAP P.66

11 Spring Hill, PO38 1PE. ☏ 01983 855407, ⓦ www.ventnorheritage.org.uk. May–Oct 10am–4pm, Sat 10am–12.30pm; Nov–April Sat only 10am–12.30pm. £2; under 16s free.

On the corner of Spring Hill is the small and replete **Heritage Centre**, featuring interesting displays, exhibits and video footage charting the small town's history, and even a model train. You can also read about notable figures who are connected with Ventnor: Charles Dickens wrote six chapters of *David Copperfield* in nearby Bonchurch, while former prime minister Winston Churchill spent time here as a young boy.

Ventnor Beach

Botanical Gardens

MAP P.66

Undercliff Drive, PO38 1UL. ☎ 01983 855397, ⓦ botanic.co.uk. Daily 10am–5pm. £9.50, under-16s £6.

You can spend the best part of a morning winding your way around the **Botanical Gardens**, whose sprawling landscape features a range of subtropical vegetation. You can thank the south-facing Undercliff for this, as it gives Ventnor its own microclimate that is similar to the Mediterranean. As such, a great variety of subtropical plants grow naturally here that wouldn't on mainland Britain. You'll also find a lovely restaurant and café on site to break the day up with.

Steephill Cove

MAP P.66

A mile east of Ventnor along the coast path, or down Love Lane (past the cricket club). There's no car access to the cove, but there's a small car park on Steephill Rd, from where it is a 5min walk down a footpath to the bay.

The former fishing hamlet of **Steephill Cove** is a lovely spot to recharge, with rock pools, a beach café and seafood restaurants to explore. Away from the noise and calamity at larger resorts, Steephil Cove gives you the chance to simply sit back and watch the fishermen at work as they have done here since the fifteenth century. The place pretty much packs up over the winter period, though, so if you plan

Ventnor Fringe Festival

Ventnor is the edgy side of the island – and we're not just talking about steep cliff faces. The six-day **Ventnor Fringe Festival** takes place at the end of July and features a delightful range of performances, from theatre and comedy to cabaret – plus cellist concerts in an eleventh-century chapel. This shows the very best that Ventnor and the island alike have to offer, and we're excited to see what happens next. For more information, head to ⓦ vfringe. co.uk.

Devil's Chimney

to visit then, come prepared with a picnic. Whatever the weather, it's a pleasant spot to wander around and take in the whitewashed cottages that roll down the rocky cliffs to the beach – which really tells you how the hamlet got its name.

Bonchurch

MAP P.66

Just over a mile east from Ventnor is **Bonchurch**, a village of thatched cottages, low-set stone edifices and Victorian houses. Despite its sleepy and secluded appearance, Bonchurch has welcomed a number of prominent figures, including Karl Marx, Charles Dickens (who wrote a great deal of *David Copperfield* here) and Irish author Henry De Vere Stacpoole, who is buried at St Boniface Church.

While you're here, the humble **St Boniface Church** makes for a charming stop-off. This medieval church is one of the few left in

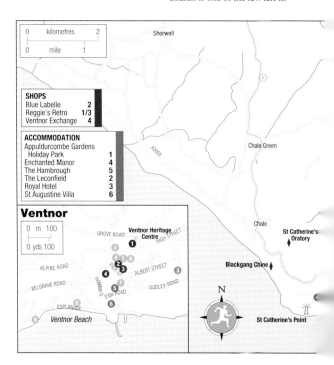

SHOPS
Blue Labelle 2
Reggie's Retro 1/3
Ventnor Exchange 4

ACCOMMODATION
Appuldurcombe Gardens
  Holiday Park 1
Enchanted Manor 4
The Hambrough 5
The Leconfield 2
Royal Hotel 3
St Augustine Villa 6

Ventnor

England of its kind, dedicated to the Saxon monk who died in 755 AD. Despite 'recent' renovations from the early twentieth century, you can still take in the Norman nave and chancel, while other aspects of the church are late Medieval, Tudor, Flemish and Romanesque. Once you've had your history fill, head down to Horseshoe Bay on the seafront, from where you can walk along to the Ventnor Esplanade.

Devil's Chimney

MAP P.66

PO38 1QD. 1min walk from Smugglers' Haven Tea Garden. Bus #3 to Landslip Car Park bus stop.

Less scarily known as Bonchurch Landslip, **Devil's Chimney** is a narrow, steep staircase cutting through the Undercliff, with *Smugglers' Haven Tea Gardens* at the top and the coastal path at the bottom – you can access from either way. There are handrails

at the steepest points, and it's advisable to tackle the deep cleft while there's plenty of daylight.

Isle of Wight Donkey Sanctuary

MAP P.66

Lower Winstone Farm, St Johns Rd, Wroxall, PO38 3AA. ☎ 01983 852693, ⊚ iwdonkey-sanctuary.com. Daily 10.30am–4.30pm. Free; donations welcome.

The main (and only) thing worth venturing to Wroxall for is the village's small **Donkey Sanctuary**, home to 97 donkeys and 26 ponies that have been rescued from unwanted homes. With 55 acres to explore, they are very well looked after. Not just a visitor attraction, the sanctuary also offers donkey therapy, work with children and more.

Appuldurcombe House

MAP P.66

Appuldurcombe Rd, Wroxall, PO38 3EW. ☎ 01983 840188, ⊚ appuldurcombe.co.uk.

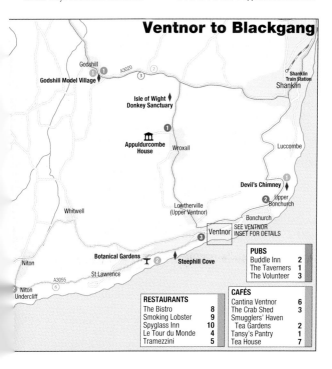

Ventnor to Blackgang

Godshill
Godshill Model Village

Shanklin Train Station
Shanklin

Isle of Wight Donkey Sanctuary

Appuldurcombe House
Wroxall

Luccombe

Devil's Chimney

Upper Bonchurch

Lowtherville (Upper Ventnor)

Bonchurch

Whitwell

Ventnor
SEE VENTNOR INSET FOR DETAILS

Niton

Botanical Gardens

Steephill Cove

St Lawrence

A3055

Niton Undercliff

PUBS	
Buddle Inn	2
The Taverners	1
The Volunteer	3

RESTAURANTS	
The Bistro	8
Smoking Lobster	9
Spyglass Inn	10
Le Tour du Monde	4
Tramezzini	5

CAFÉS	
Cantina Ventnor	6
The Crab Shed	3
Smugglers' Haven Tea Gardens	2
Tansy's Pantry	1
Tea House	7

Godshill Model Village

April–Sept Sun–Fri 10am–5pm. Free.
Just half a mile from the village
of Wroxall and surrounded by
tumbling fields of countryside
is **Appuldurcombe House**, an
eighteenth-century house that once
sat in the Worsley family. With its
Palladian-style exterior, renovated
Great Hall and landscaped gardens
(designed by Lancelot 'Capability'
Brown), it's one of the most
magnificent English Heritage
sites on the island. An accidental
landmine hit the site during World
War II, but the largest thing to
hit the house was the notorious
Worsley Scandal, where in 1782,
Mrs Worsley admitted to having
had 27 lovers – the details of the
scandal became something of a
bestseller.

Godshill

MAP P.66
Buses #2 and #3.
Godshill appears as a model village
itself, with quaint teahouses,
thatched cottages and a medieval
church setting itself as what many
regard as the prettiest village on the
island. On the high street, **The Old
Smithy** provides a range of shops
and cafés in numerous historic

buildings. To make the most of
the outdoors, check out the ornate
garden behind the Old Smithy, and
there's also a Model Village (see
below).

Godshill Model Village

MAP P.66
**High St, PO38 3HH. ☎ 01983 840270,
Ⓦ www.modelvillagegodshill.co.uk. March
10am–4pm; April–mid July, Sept & Oct
10am–5pm; late-July & Aug 10am–6pm.
Adult £5.95, under 16s £5.25. Buses #2
and #3.**
Everyone will appreciate the
intricate details at the **Model
Village**, with its displays of
1920s Shanklin and Godshill in
micro-form. There are also detailed
landscape gardens featuring over
3000 shrubs and plants.

St Catherine's Point

MAP P.66
**£5, under 16s £3: cash only. Ⓦ www.trinity
house.co.uk/lighthouse-visitor-centres/st-
catherines-lighthouse-visitor-centre. Closed
in 2020; check website for reopening times.**
The Undercliff recedes at Niton,
a village in Ventnor just along
the way from St Lawrence.
Built in 1838, the lighthouse
at **St Catherine's Point**, the

southernmost tip of the island, stands at 27m tall and takes 94 steps to reach the top. Tours are available if booked in advance and last roughly 40mins, but note that at the time of writing, the octagonal white lighthouse was confirmed to be closed throughout 2020. Not to worry, though – you can stretch your legs with a stroll along St Catherine's Down or head down to clumpy Reeth Bay.

St Catherine's Oratory

MAP P.66

Blackgang Road, Chale, PO38 2JB. Free; EH. ⓦ www.english-heritage.org.uk/visit/places/st-catherines-oratory.

Walk along the roves of fields and past grazing cows on the cliff to **St Catherine's Oratory**, also known as the Pepperpot. Once used as a lighthouse, this medieval tower is all that remains of an oratory that was built in 1328, where a local landowner kept casks of white wine from a nearby shipwreck. Not far from the lighthouse at St Catherine's

Point; it's located on one of the highest points of the island.

Blackgang Chine

MAP P.66

Blackgang, PO38 2HN. ☎ 01983 730330, ⓦ blackgangchine.com. Daily: mid-March to mid-Sept 10am–5pm or 6pm; mid-Sept to Oct 10am–4.30pm; stays open later some nights in summer hols and Oct half-term. £20.

The awesome **Blackgang Chine** theme park lies just two miles west on Niton's clifftop. There are rides and attractions that will suit every age here, from the screech-inducing Cliffhanger roller-coaster to the jiggling Pirate Barrels. The different themes of the park include Cowboy Town, Underwater Kingdom, Fairyland and Pirate Cove, where kids can let their imaginations (and themselves) run wild. There are regular performances from 'Blackgang's Characters' which will keep everyone entertained – and in one place.

Tip-toe trails around Niton

There's an excellent **trail** you can take that covers 3.5 miles (5.6km). This route will see you take in an ever-changing view of the wildlife and coast, and takes between two and two and a half hours to complete, although there's plenty of benches along the way. It's a fairly **moderate walk** with strenuous and steep sections, so make sure you wear suitable footwear.

The route starts at the **Old Blackgang Road car park** at the Niton undercliff, where you'll pass along a grassy track. Follow through the valley until you reach **Knowles Farm** (check out the memorial plaque to electrical engineer and inventor Marconi). Keep to the edge as safely as possible along the **lighthouse**, through Castlehaven caravan park, and turn left at the stony track. The route then ascends uphill with the assistance of steps and a handrail, which leads you to opposite the *Buddle Inn* pub. Once you've checked for any oncoming traffic, take the coast path up Barrack Shute and towards **Niton village**. Then, take a left at the marker post, but note that the path gets narrow and pretty slippy here, so take care. Turn right, follow the road back to the **Sandrock Road car park** and you've made it!

For more information, visit the ever-helpful National Trust website or use the OS Maps: Landranger 196, Explorer OL29 to guide you with more detail.

Shops

Blue Labelle

MAP P.66

7 Pier St, PO38 1ST. ☎ 01983 700878, Ⓦ bluelabelle.co.uk. Tues 9am–4.30pm, Wed–Sat 10.30am–4.30pm.

Blue Labelle is a small boutique in Ventnor, who make and sell their own skincare products. Skincare creams and oils are all organic and vegan. There's also a small selection of stocked local products, too: think candles, local art and upcycled bags.

Reggie's Retro

MAP P.66

Bookshop 9 Spring Hill, PO38 1PE; clothing store 15 Pier St, PO38 1ST. ☎ 07966 303354/716654, Ⓦ www.facebook.com/reggiesretroclothing & Ⓦ www.facebook.com/reggiesretro. Pier St store Mon–Sat 10am–5pm, Spring Hill Store Wed–Fri 11am–5pm & 10am–5pm.

Spread across two stores, *Reggie's Retro* specialises in vintage books, records and fashion from all eras: it's a true emporium of items, and is a key social spot in Ventnor, too. The shop owners

Pier Street

are more than happy to chat or let you browse at your own leisure – and proves Ventnor as an innovative, independent and valued community.

Ventnor Exchange

MAP P.66

11 Church St, PO38 1SW. ☎ 01983 716767, Ⓦ ventnorexchange.co.uk. Tues–Sat noon–11pm.

Part-theatre, craft beer bar and record shop, the *Ventnor Exchange* is a creative space promoting the best of the community. They put on the Ventnor Fringe Festival each year (see page 65) as well as regular shows, workshops and events. You can choose to chill out with a drink and flick through the vinyls on sale – you might even stumble across a *Rough Guide to Psychedelia*.

Restaurants

The Bistro

MAP P.66

30 Pier St, PO 1SX. ☎ 01983 853334, Ⓦ www.thebistroventnor.co.uk. Wed–Sat 10am–2pm & 6–9pm, Sun noon–2pm.

Not far from the steep ascent (or descent) to the Esplanade, *The Bistro* uses an abundance of local ingredients in their regularly changing brunch, lunch and dinner menus, from brie and cranberry ciabatta (£6.50) to baked hake fillet (£21). Their 'open kitchen' means you can watch chefs prepare your meal, all of which is served in a relaxed ambience with contemporary artwork to match. It's worth reserving a table.

Smoking Lobster

MAP P.66

Esplanade, PO38 1JT. ☎ 01983 855938, Ⓦ smokinglobster.co.uk/. Noon–11pm.

Island-famous restaurant serving contemporary Asian dishes along the Esplanade. Tuck into whole ginger and soy baked sea bass (£24), surf & turf (from £36) and

Spyglass Inn

other grilled items such as fillet steak with chimichurri (£26). Their slick, white interior overlooks the beach and out across the sea, and there's outside dining during the warmer months.

Spyglass Inn

MAP P.66

Ventnor Esplanade, Ventnor, PO38 1JX ☏ 01983 855338, Ⓦ thespyglass.com. Once a Victorian bath house, this lively pub on the seafront offers pub grub (homemade fisherman's pie £14.25), regular live music and is jam-packed with smuggling memorabilia.

Le Tour du Monde

MAP P.66

11 High St, Ventnor ☏ 01983 854355, Ⓦ www.letourdumonde.co.uk. Daily 6–9pm.

Seeing as you're so close to France, it's worth dining here, formerly *Fogg's of Ventnor*. This French restaurant includes starters like mushrooms in tarragon cream sauce on crusty bread (£7.95), mains like venison steak (£22.50) and a homemade dessert of red wine-poached pears (£7.50). They

also sell handmade chocolates and truffles (such as Cranberry ganache marinated in cognac), which are available to take away.

Tramezzini

MAP P.66

14 High St, PO38 1RZ. ☏ 01983 855510, Ⓦ tramezzini.co.uk. Lunch: Mon–Sat 8am–3pm; Dinner: Thurs–Sat 6pm–late. Run by two passionate, international chefs, *Tramezzini* offers it all: for breakfast, go for poached eggs and pancetta on toast (£5.50); lunch, pan-fried catch of the day (£18); and for dinner, opt for scallop and cuttlefish ink linguine (£18).

Cafés

Cantina Ventnor

MAP P.66

Bonchurch Village Rd, Bonchurch, PO38 1RG ☏ 01983 855988, Ⓦ cantinaventnor. co.uk. Daily 7.30am–10pm. Excellent café-bakery and restaurant, which also serves cocktails (Earl Grey martini £7). Brunch is served all day (think *shakshuka* £7 or the full works £8.50) – while dinner is

The Crab Shed

served from 6pm, offering a range of small plates, large mains, pizzas and desserts.

The Crab Shed

MAP P.66

Steephill Cove, PO38 1AF. ① 01983 855819, ⓦ www.steephillcove-isleofwight.co.uk/crab_shed.html. April–Sept Mon & Wed–Sun noon–3pm, weather dependent. Delicious home-made crab pasties and fresh mackerel served from a pretty shack with outdoor seats on the seashore. Their seafood is caught just metres away, down at Steephill Cove – keep an eye out for the fishermen bringing their haul up.

Smugglers' Haven Tea Gardens

MAP P.66

76 Leeson Rd, PO38 1QD. ① 01983 852992. Daily 10am–4.30pm. Hidden away but delightful to find, this wholesome, tranquil spot in Bonchurch offers no-frills food like beans on toast and fresh crab sandwiches at fairly reasonable prices. They have tables outside with amazing views of the Channel and makes for a good reward after climbing the Devil's Chimney (see page 67). Veggie and vegan options also available.

Tansy's Pantry

MAP P.66

Church Hollow, Godshill, PO38 3HH. ① 01983 840921, ⓦ tansyspantry.co.uk. Lunch: Tues–Sat 10am–4pm; Dinner: Thurs & Fri 5.30–10pm. This restaurant-café serves up plant-based, vegan options; the menu includes the likes of "soul bowls" (£9.95), 'vish' and chips (£11.95) and a banging Tansy's Burger. Gluten-free options are also available, as are vegan wines, beers and ciders.

Tea House

MAP P.66

40 High St, PO38 1RZ. ① 01983 856478, ⓦ www.theteahouseventnor.co.uk. Tues–Sun 8am–5pm. All very vintage, all very Ventnor here at the *Tea House*. Expect vintage record plates, delicate bone china and urban-vintage furniture.

Serves sandwiches (from £3.75), hot breakfasts (avocado, mushroom and spinach on toast £7.75), or simply pop in for a toasted teacake with a cup of loose leaf tea or island-roasted coffee.

Pubs

Buddle Inn

MAP P.66

St Catherine's Rd, PO38 2NE. ☎ 01983 730243, Ⓦ buddleinn.co.uk. Wed & Thurs noon–9pm, Fri & Sat noon–10pm, Sun noon–6pm; food served until an hour before closing.

The *Buddle Inn* is riddled with traditional charm, from flagstone floors to rustic inglenook beams and crackling fires in between the two. This sixteenth-century restaurant-pub is set in the island's Area of Outstanding Natural Beauty and as such serves a range of real ales and extensive homemade dishes with a view – just head out to the garden area which looks out to the sea.

The Taverners

MAP P.66

The Buddle Inn

High St, Godshill, PO38 3HZ. ☎ 01983 840707, Ⓦ thetavernersgodshill.co.uk. Mon–Thurs noon–2.45pm & 6–8.45pm, Fri & Sat noon–2.45pm & 6–9.15pm, Sun noon–2.45pm.

A proper country pub with food foraged, caught or bought each day – they also bake their own bread and use local, seasonal ingredients year-round. Pub favourites include pork sausages with bubble and squeak (£10.95) and Taverners Ploughman's (£7.95), with a lengthy wine list to boot.

The Volunteer

MAP P.66

30 Victoria St, PO38 1ES. ☎ 01983 852537. Ⓦ www.facebook.com/The-Volunteer-386954771421365.

No, you haven't barged into someone's living room, it's just possibly the town's smallest pub. It's a very welcoming, sociable space, as all great pubs should be, but it is pretty tiny, so not suitable for larger groups or families. There's a small games room at the back, live music on Sundays and a selection of fine real ales.

Brighstone to Alum Bay

The southwest coast is one of the least-populated areas of the island, and as a whole is largely undeveloped; there's no doubting why it forms part of a designated Area of Outstanding Natural Beauty (AONB). This is what makes it such prime walking and cycling territory, with Compton Bay and Freshwater Bay to cool off at. There's a built up development around Freshwater and Totland, the western tip of the island, but head out further to the westernmost tip for some of the best-known and rugged views of the rugged island. You can enjoy this from either up high or down low: the multicoloured sand cliffs of Alum Bay, the jagged spine-like Needles and the sweeping views from the top of the headland. To make even more of the great outdoors, you can walk along the superlative Tennyson Down, where the poet Lord Tennyson once frequented. Brighstone is set in the rolling countryside, and is within walking distance from the captivating gardens at the National Trust-owned Mottistone.

Brighstone

MAP P.76

The compact village of **Brighstone** is filled with low thatched cottages, the most stand-out of which can be viewed on North Street, which are owned by the National Trust. This genteel village is set just a little further inland from the unspoilt beach at Brighstone Bay, so you can get the wind out your ears with its leafy

Mottistone Gardens & Estate

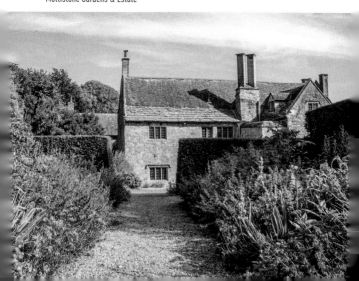

lanes and slower pace of life; it's all part of the island's AONB.

Brighstone Museum

MAP P.76

North St, Brighstone, PO30 4AX. Tues 9am–12.30pm, Thurs 1.30–4.30pm, Sat 10am–4pm. Free.

In one of the converted cottages lies **Brighstone Museum**, which provides a detailed insight into village life. It's a small space, but they bring traditional village life in Brighstone to life with a recreated Victorian cottage kitchen, themed displays and audio recordings of villagers reflecting on their childhoods spent growing up here.

Mottistone Gardens & Estate

MAP P.76

Mottistone, PO30 4EA. ⊕ 01983 741302, ⊕ nationaltrust.org.uk/mottistone-gardens. Mid-March to Oct Mon–Thurs & Sun 10.30am–5pm. Free; NT.

Six acres of formal, terraced gardens with a burst of colourful flowers await you at **Mottistone Gardens & Estate**. Located three miles or so west of Brighstone, the peaceful gardens are part of a 650-acre estate, surrounding an Elizabethan manor house. Bringing it ever-so slightly up to date is the Art Deco cabin 'Shack', once a former architects office but now, much more aptly, an organic kitchen garden and tea garden. Among the flora on display here are olive groves, shrub-filled banks and exotic plants.

Tapnell Farm

MAP P.76

Tapnell Farm, Newport Rd, PO41 0YJ.

Brighstone village

⊕ 01983 758722, ⊕ tapnellfarm.com. Daily 10am–4.30pm. £7.50, under-16s £9.50.

At **Tapnell Farm** you can meet the animals, tackle a climbing wall and whizz down the sledge slides, alongside plenty of other activities. There are wallabies and meerkats, alpacas and farmyard animals to interact with; the farm is also home to a variety of accommodation types. A brand-new Aqua Park should have opened by the time you're reading this; check ⊕ tapnellfarm.com/aquapark for updates.

Farringford

MAP P.76

Bedbury Lane, Freshwater Bay, PO40 9PE. ⊕ 01983 752500, ⊕ farringford.co.uk. April–Oct Wed–Fri:

Coastal trail: Colwell Bay to Totland Bay

Start at Colwell Bay at *The Hut*, a beachfront café popular with passing celebs. The concrete trail will see you pass colourful beach huts on your left and views of Bournemouth on your right. It takes about 15mins to reach Totland Bay, before ending the route with lunch or a drink at *The Waterfront*, a pleasant restaurant overlooking the Bay.

House tours 10.15am, 11.45am, 2.45pm and 3.15pm, Gardens 10am–4.30pm. House tours £11.50, under 17s £6.50, gardens £3.50, under 17s £2.
Historic-house-turned-hotel, **Farringford** was the main residence of Lord Tennyson between 1856 to 1892, and remained in Tennyson family possession until 1945. Today, you can take guided house tours of this Grade I-listed building, as well as a visit to the well-kept gardens. Pre-booking onto a house tour is advised.

Dimbola Lodge

MAP P.76
Terrace Lane, Freshwater Bay, PO40 9QE.
☏ 01983 756814, ⓦ dimbola.co.uk.
April–Sept 10am–4pm; tearoom until 3pm. £6.

While many are happy to dive into Freshwater Bay and schlep along Tennyson Down, few think to travel a little further inland from the Bay. They'll miss out on

Dimbola Lodge, the house-turned-museum of pioneering Victorian photographer Julia Margaret Cameron. After visiting friend Lord Tennyson here in Freshwater in 1860, she moved to this spot – right by the public footpath entrance to the Tennyson Down – and today you can marvel at the same views as she once did. Inside the house, the rooms are arranged by photographs of her various contemporaries, from Charles Darwin to Robert Browning. Aside from Julia's work there are also displays and items regarding the history of photography, her reconstructed bedroom and a colourful chronicle of the Isle of Wight festival, including some bare-bottomed hippies (photographed, that is). Once you've finished mooching around, head back downstairs to their tearoom for a pleasant view over the Downs and sea ahead.

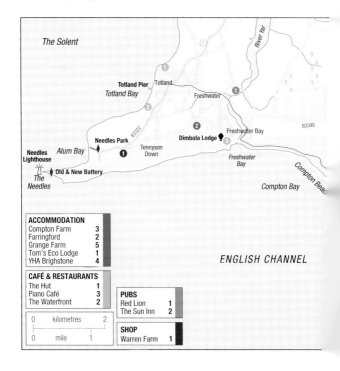

ACCOMMODATION
Compton Farm	3
Farringford	2
Grange Farm	5
Tom's Eco Lodge	1
YHA Brighstone	4

CAFÉ & RESTAURANTS
The Hut	1
Piano Café	3
The Waterfront	2

PUBS
| Red Lion | 1 |
| The Sun Inn | 2 |

SHOP
| Warren Farm | 1 |

Tennyson Down

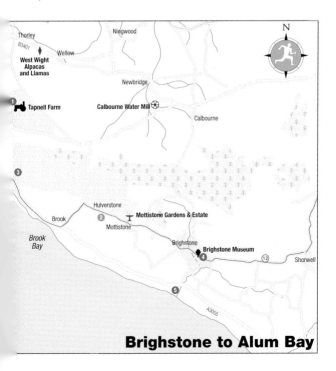

Brighstone to Alum Bay

Tennyson Down

MAP P.76

Tennyson Down was named after the Victorian poet Alfred Tennyson, who resided in Freshwater after relocating from London. He enjoyed walking across the downs (who wouldn't?) and today there stands a monument to him at the highest point of the clifftop, a marble Celtic cross. And what an idyllic stretch of downs to bear your name, with its strong gusts of salt air, cliff-nesting birds and copious pinpricks of wildflowers. There's a well-marked path you can follow that leads onto the Needles. Dogs are welcome on leads, as there's various livestock and wildlife gradually being reintroduced to the Downs.

Alum Bay

MAP P.76

Alum Bay sits at the island's western tip and is one of the most picturesque spots on the island, with a view of the Needles in the near-distance. The multi-coloured sand cliffs, for which the area is known (and where Victorian locals got their paint pigments from) consist of three minerals (quarts, felspar and mica), due to millions of years' worth of seabeds rising, eroding and sinking beneath the sea, and bedrocks causing these sediments to form the cliffs you see today. An Alum Bay sand-filled glass jar makes for a fun souvenir.

Needles Park

MAP P.76

Alum Bay, PO39 OJD. ⓦ theneedles.co.uk. Easter–Oct daily 10am–4pm, later some days in summer. Free; chairlift £6 return. At the top of the cliff is **Needles Park**, which consists of various attractions suitable for children. More will enjoy the views to be had from the **chairlift** at the cliff down to Alum Bay. Aside from the attractions, the Needles Park is a good place to enjoy a picnic, otherwise there are a couple of shops and cafés to enjoy the views from.

Old Battery

MAP P.76

West High Down, PO39 OJH. ☎ 01983 754772, ⓦ nationaltrust.org.uk/needles-old-battery-and-new-battery. Mid-March to Oct daily 10.30am–5pm. £6.85, children £3.45; NT.

The Needles and Alum Bay

The link to the mainland

The Needles are three jagged chalk stacks that jut out of the island's western headland at 30m high. There was a fourth stack, but this collapsed during a colossal storm in 1764 – its rumblings were thought to have been heard in Portsmouth. Although you can't see it, the chalk spine continues underneath the sea floor and emerges again at Dorset's Isle of Purbeck. If you stand at the top of either site, you'll see how the two were once connected.

Thousands of years ago, the sea levels changed, and erosion caused upheaval which disconnected the island from the mainland. Before the Isle of Wight became an island, what is now the Solent (the stretch of sea between the island the mainland), was the River Solent; this huge stretch of saltwater now separated the island from the mainland.

Stretch your legs to the lookout at **Old Battery**, a Victorian coastal defence fort. Built to defend Britain from French invasion, the fort was also in use during both world wars. Also here are the remains of the original lighthouse (dating back to 1786) that once warned incoming sailors about the rocky outcrops. Modern-day sailors needn't worry, as it has since been replaced with a 'new' (1859, that is) one at the end of the Needles, its red and white hoops vivid against the white chalk stacks.

New Battery

MAP P.76

☏ 01983 754772, ⓦ nationaltrust.org.uk/needles-old-battery-and-new-battery. Mid-March to Oct daily 11am–4pm. Free.

The **New Battery** was built in 1895 as a replacement for the Old Battery – where there had been concerns about its position causing the cliffs to crumble – and was built higher up the cliff and 120m above sea level. It then went onto become a top-secret military rocket-testing site between 1955 and 1971 (during the Cold War); following this, it become a significant site for researching early space technology, and in 1971 the single all-British satellite was launched into orbit.

Totland

MAP P.76

The next bay on from Alum Bay is **Totland Bay**, which you can walk along via its seafront promenade. As you walk north towards Compton Bay, the northern views of the mainland (Bournemouth) creep into view. You'll have to head inland before coming down onto the bay by the *Waterfront* restaurant.

Compton Bay

MAP P.76

Sunbathe on the sand or lay back on the grassy clifftop at **Compton Bay**. West of Brighstone, this is one of the lesser-developed parts of the island, but that doesn't mean it's any less busy. With its crashing waves and perfect location, it's a popular spot with surfers, bodyboarders and anyone else who wants to make the most of the waves.

This is also one of the best spots to find dinosaur fossils; there are the three-toed footprints of Iguanodon between 985–1968ft wide at the cliff base east of Compton Bay car park at Hanover Point. Tours and walks can be organized – see ⓦ visitisleofwight.co.uk for more information.

Shop

Warren Farm

MAP P.76

Alum Bay New Rd, PO39 0JB. ☎ 01983 753200, ⓦ warrenfarmiow.co.uk. Summer only.

Lovely family-run farm (for over 50 years) with a farm shop and tea gardens. They produce beef from their own herd of Hereford cross cows that graze the fields, with the Needles as a backdrop on their 150-acre farm. Their outdoor seating overlooks the equally pleasant Tennyson Down, but there's also covered seating. Take a respite here after a visit to the Needles and enjoy their variety of hot and cold drinks, cakes, snacks – then buy some of the local produce (including eggs, cheese or their own beef) to take home or as a gift.

Restaurants

The Hut

MAP P.76

Colwell Bay, PO40 9NP. ☎ 01983 898637, ⓦ thehutcolwell.co.uk. April–Oct Tues–Sat

Diners at *The Hut*

11am–midnight, Sun 11am–5pm.
Upmarket beachfront restaurant popular with celebrities, serving a seafood-heavy menu such as tuna poke bowls (£15), shellfish spaghetti (£18), or push the boat out with grilled lobster (£45).

The Waterfront

MAP P.76

Totland Bay, PO39 0BQ. ☎ 01983 756969, ⓦ www.waterfrontiow.com. Mon–Thurs 11am–10pm, Fri & Sat 11am–11pm, Sun 11am–7pm.

Restaurant with amazing views over Totland Bay. The building previously served as a church, reading room and library. It now serves a mixture of Mediterranean and British foods, alongside a bar, with live music on Fri and Sat nights.

Café

Piano Café

MAP P.76

Gate Lane, Freshwater, PO40 9PY. ☎ 01983 472874, ⓦ thepianocafe.co.uk. Feb–Dec Tues–Thurs 8.30am–4pm, Fri & Sat till 10pm, Sun 9am–5pm.

The Red Lion

Queen Victoria's piano tuner once owned the building, hence its appropriate name. it's now a stylishly decorated café, bar and meze restaurant. They serve meals (from £6.75) throughout the day, including hot and cold meze options and sharing platters. There's also monthly live music nights, and a variety of other events.

Pubs

Red Lion
MAP P.76

Church Place, Freshwater, PO40 9BP. ☎ 01983 754925, Ⓦ www.redlion-freshwater.co.uk. Pub Mon–Sat 11am–11pm, Sun 11am–10.30pm, kitchen daily noon–2.30pm & 6–9pm.

This attractive traditional pub has log fires, real ales and a lovely big garden. Choose from an award-winning menu; freshly beer-battered fish of the day costs £11.

The Sun Inn
MAP P.76

Hulverstone, PO30 4EH ☎ 01983 741124, Ⓦ sunhulverstone.co.uk. Tues–Thurs noon–9pm, Fri & Sat until 10pm, Sun until 6pm; food served until an hour earlier.

A cosy, dog-friendly pub with a thatched roof and a garden. It serves local and slightly different pub food, such as duck lasagne (£14) and island steak & Fuggle-Dee-Dum (a local ale) pie (£13.50).

Yarmouth and around

The northwestern town of Yarmouth sits at the mouth of the River Yar and makes for an attractive arrival point to the island. Originally known as Eremue ("muddy estuary"), the settlement is one of the oldest on the island, dating back to at least 991, with a Norman grid system still in place. Yarmouth is encompassed by a river one side and marshland the other, with the sea looking north towards the mainland. It's an ideal starting point to venture to the likes of ancient Newtown and the trickling-stream village of Calbourne, which is slightly further inland. Yarmouth itself has a good selection of places to eat, drink and stay, but it's tightly knitted with a village square-like feel, so it won't take you too long to explore. However, you'll soon be drawn to its beguiling history and will find it easy to nestle in with the village-like community. This is somewhere you'll want to linger, or at least consider returning to for a pleasant day trip; Yarmouth is linked to Lymington in the New Forest by car ferry, which pulls in alongside the picturesque marina.

View over Yarmouth

Yarmouth Pier

Yarmouth Castle

MAP P.87

Quay St, PO41 0PB. ☏ 01983 760678, ⓦ www.english-heritage.org.uk/visit/places/yarmouth-castle. April–Oct Wed–Sun 11am–4pm. £5.70, under-17s £3.40; EH.

Yarmouth Castle, the last and most sophisticated of Henry VIII's coastal defence forts, was intended to protect the island from French invasion. The town was the main port on the island and had been burnt down by them twice before. However, the fort was only completed in 1574, 33 years after his death. Today, you can look around the inside of this sixteenth-century castle, with reconstructed rooms explaining how they were used at the time, as well as displays of various Solent shipwrecks. There are some spectacular estuary views to be had from the battlements.

Yarmouth Pier

MAP P.87

PO41 0NP. Year-round. 50p.

The longest wooden bridge in England still in use, this Victorian-era **pier** still makes for a nice stroll, with views across the deep water to the mainland; as you walk back, take in the views of the fancy waterfront houses on your left, clinking yacht masts from the marina on your right and chunky Red Funnel ferry entering and leaving harbour. There's a small hut at the end of the pier detailing its history as well as information about local sealife.

Fort Victoria Country Park

MAP P.84.

West Hill Lane, PO41 0RR. ☏ 01983 823893, ⓦ www.fortvictoria.co.uk. See website for individual prices and times. Bus # then a 10min walk, or 20min walk along coastal path.

Explore the peaceful walks of the country park and along the seashore, or visit the Reptilarium, planetarium, archeology centre and café under the arches of **Fort Victoria**, a former military fort which once protected Portsmouth and Bournemouth (and the rest of England) from attack from the Spanish Armada.

Newtown Old Town Hall

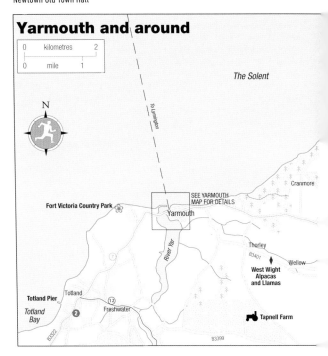

Yarmouth and around

The Solent

To Lymington

SEE YARMOUTH
MAP FOR DETAILS

Fort Victoria Country Park

Yarmouth

Cranmore

River Yar

Thorley

B3401

West Wight
Alpacas
and Llamas

Wellow

Totland Pier

Totland

Freshwater

Totland
Bay

B3322

Tapnell Farm

B3399

West Wight Alpacas and Llamas

MAP P.84

Bus #7 to West Wight Alpacas stop. Main Road, Wellow, PO41 0SZ. ☎ 01983 760900, ⓦ www.westwightalpacas.co.uk. Daily 10am–5pm. Adults £7.50, children £5, under 4s free.

There are alpacas, llamas, pygmy goats, miniature donkeys, rare breed sheep, pigs, rabbits and more at the **farm** here. You can take walks, give lamb feeding a go, or go 'cria (baby alpaca)-watching'. There's also a bistro and pizzeria onsite, where you can sample artisan wood-fired pizzas using local ingredients from the farm.

Newtown

MAP P.84

Newtown is little more than a peaceful village – but that wasn't always the case. For 150 years it served as the island's capital, and one of the few remains of its significant past is the Jacobean **town hall** (ⓦ nationaltrust.org.uk/newtown-old-town-hall), except there's no actual town surrounding it. The other remain is a trace of its gridded street pattern, but that's about it. Dating back to the thirteenth century, Newtown is also home to a nature reserve, one of the best spots for bird-watching in the UK. If you've explored all that Yarmouth has to offer then make the four-mile journey across to here, where there are pleasant walks to be had around the nature reserve, with footpaths, a jetty and flower-covered salt marshes.

Newtown Old Town Hall

MAP P.84

Town Lane, PO30 4PA. ☎ 01983 531622, ⓦ nationaltrust.org.uk/newtown-old-town-hall. Only open four days a year in May and Sept at 2pm and 3pm; see website for details. £4.30; children. £2.15; NT members free.

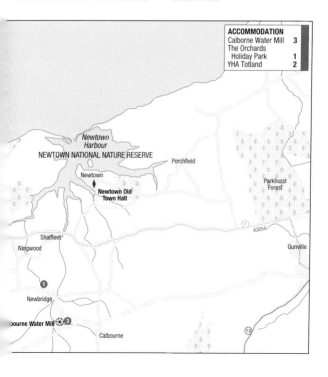

ACCOMMODATION	
Calborne Water Mill	3
The Orchards Holiday Park	1
YHA Totland	2

Newtown National Nature Reserve

MAP P.84
Free

The **Newtown National Nature Reserve** is little changed: its field patterns reflect its Medieval origins. It's also the only such reserve on the island, with harbourside and woodland walks, carpets of meadows and tall grass, and an abundance of wildlife. In the 1960s, there was a threat of it becoming a nuclear power station; but with local intervention, who proved how significant its local wildlife was, it was left as you see it today.

Calbourne Water Mill

MAP P.84
Westover, Calbourne, PO30 4JN. ☎ 01983 531227, ⓦ calbournewatermill.co.uk. March–Nov daily 10am–5pm. £10; under 16s £6.

Five miles southeast of Yarmouth lies the charming village of **Calbourne**. One of its most picturesque streets is Winkle Street, a line of thatched cottages blanketed with green ivy overlooking the trickling stream. Another mile outside of the village is **Calbourne Water Mill,** which is included in the historic Domesday Book and is the oldest working water mill on the island. Things to do and see here include milling demonstrations, feeding the peacocks and hiring a punt on the mill stream.

Newtown Nature Reserve

The red-brick National Trust **Old Town Hall** dates all the way back to 1699, and is the only remaining evidence of the town's former importance – this was where difficult elections were held and saw two Members sent to Parliament. Nowadays, it's set in an open, grassy space that forms part of the Nature Reserve. They also have the notorious Ferguson's Gang to thank for their preservation – see box for more details.

Meet Ferguson's Gang

You probably haven't heard of **The Ferguson's Gang**; a notorious 'gang' of five women who formed in 1927 to raise awareness and funds for the National Trust. They were passionate about protecting and preserving important buildings and land under threat – one of their acts included purchasing **Newtown Old Town Hall** which they then gave to the National Trust. Although they used pseudonyms to remain anonymous, they received UK-wide press coverage for their outlandish ways of sending donations, like delivering the 'swag' inside a fake pineapple. You can read about their exploits in a small book that's on display at the Old Town Hall.

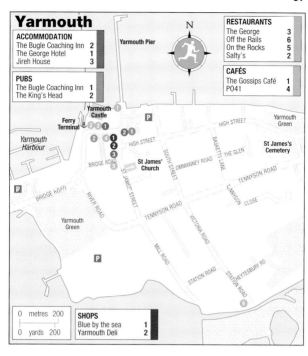

Yarmouth

ACCOMMODATION
The Bugle Coaching Inn	2
The George Hotel	1
Jireh House	3

PUBS
The Bugle Coaching Inn	1
The King's Head	2

RESTAURANTS
The George	3
Off the Rails	6
On the Rocks	5
Salty's	2

CAFÉS
The Gossips Café	1
PO41	4

SHOPS
Blue by the sea	1
Yarmouth Deli	2

Winkle Street, Calbourne

88

YARMOUTH AND AROUND

Shops

Blue by the sea
MAP P.87
Quay St, PO41 0PB. ☎ 01983 760362,
Ⓦ www.bluebythesea.co.uk. Mon–Sat
10am–5pm, Sun 11am–4pm.
Boutique store selling clothing,
homemade local jewellery and
niche coastal-themed items. Take
a seat if they're free – otherwise
the owner's two dogs are probably
napping there.

Yarmouth Deli
MAP P.87
1 The Square, PO41 0NS. ☎ 01983 761196.
Daily 8.30am–5.30pm.
Set in the little village square, this
local produce shop is a great place
to pack up on picnic supplies, from
frittatas and pork pies to olives
and eggs.

Restaurants

The George
MAP P.87
☎ 01983 760331, Ⓦ www.thegeorge.co.uk/
dining.

The George

Dine at the brasserie-
style restaurant out in the
Conservatory, with breakfast,
lunch and dinner served daily.
Expect great food – the chef also
runs *Thompson's* in Newport (see
page 42) – offering summer
and winter menus, and a two-
course set menu at £20.

Off the Rails
MAP P.87
Station Rd, PO41 0QX. ☎ 01983 761600,
Ⓦ www.offtherailsyarmouth.co.uk. Wed–
Sun 9am–4pm, Sat also 6–10pm.
This unique restaurant is set along
the line of Yarmouth's old train
station. Pop in for a bacon roll
(£6.50) for breakfast, tuck into a
beef burger in a charcoal bun (£16)
or feast on slow-cooked lamb stew
(£19).

On the Rocks
MAP P.87
Bridge Rd, PO41 0PJ. ☎ 01983 760505,
Ⓦ www.ontherocksyarmouth.com. Daily
6–11pm.
As the name suggests, everything
on the menu here is served on a
sizzling hot rock plate. Choose
from the likes of steak, chicken,

seafood and halloumi (generally between £18 and £22), served with bread, Greek salad and julienne fries.

Salty's

MAP P.87

Quay St, PO41 0PB. ☎ 01983 761550, Ⓦ www.saltysrestaurant.co.uk. May–Nov Tues–Thurs 11am–11pm, Fri 11am–11.30pm, Sat 11am–midnight, Sun 11am–6pm.

Fun, lively restaurant a stone's throw from the harbourfront. The jovial downstairs bar features long bench tables and a Mediterranean feel, while upstairs is a more formal affair serving the likes of pan-fried skate wing (£22) and 'posh surf & turf' (fillet steak and half garlic lobster £50). Their wine list also recommends pre- and post-dinner wines.

Cafés

The Gossips Café

MAP P.87

The Square, PO41 0NS. ☎ 01983 760646, Ⓦ thegossipscafe.com. Mon–Thurs 9am–4.30pm, Fri 9am–5.30pm, Sat & Sun 9am–5pm.

Conveniently located next to the pier, this coffee shop serves sandwiches, salads, stone-baked pizzas and crab specialities, as well as a range of soft, hot and alcoholic drinks. The interior is slick, airy and spacious, and outdoor seating is also available.

PO41

MAP P.87

St James Court, Quay St, PO41 0PB. ☎ 01983 761105, Ⓦ www.facebook.com/ PO41CoffeeHouse. Daily 7.30am–4pm.

Small, independent coffee shop that fills up quickly, serving freshly roasted coffee and light lunches. Their roastery is actually based in a young offenders prison, HMP Feltham Young Offenders Institute, with a mission to train the inmates coffee roasting and barista skills.

The King's Head

Pubs

The Bugle Coaching Inn

MAP P.87

The Square, PO41 0NS. ☎ 01983 760272, Ⓦ www.characterinns.co.uk/the-bugle-coaching-inn. Mon–Sat 11am–11pm, Sun until 10pm; food served daily noon–9pm.

A charming pub popular with locals, yachties and their dogs; they also serve hearty mains including fish and chips and a vegan mushroom burger (both £11.95) and smaller bites, like brie and beetroot bruschetta (£6.95). Upstairs accommodation is available.

The King's Head

MAP P.87

Quay St, PO41 0PB. ☎ 01983 760177, Ⓦ www.characterinns.co.uk/the-kings-head. Tues–Thurs noon–9pm, Fri & Sat noon–11pm, Sun noon–6pm.

Lovely pub with low-timbered ceiling, offering hearty pub classics like smoked mackerel parfait (£7.50), minted lamb pie (£13.50) and cider and leek mussels (£14).

Further afield

It can be easy to forget that there's a world outside of the Isle of Wight. The mainland points that provide transport links with the island – Portsmouth, Lymington and Southampton – all lie along the south coast and are each worth exploring in their own right; or you can easily add it on as a visit to the beginning or end of your trip to the Isle of Wight. After all, a visit to the Isle of Wight embraces slow travel, which will leave you wondering what all the rush is for, so there's no better way to continue this than by taking the time to explore these south coast towns and cities. They are filled with ancient forests, historic ruins, trendy dining spots and long stretches of beach, to name a few, and serve as a great base to explore further by foot or public transport. From the fauna of the New Forest to the family-friendly festivals in Southsea, you could happily spend a couple of extra nights on the mainland as a precursor or way to round-off your visit to the Isle of Wight. Portsmouth is well worth at least a weekend to revel in its fascinating naval history, enjoy a slice of cake in its quirky tearooms and get to grips with the local pub scene, while Southampton provides a great shopping and dining experience, and Lymington and the New Forest is the perfect way to stay reconnected with nature, wildlife and the great outdoors.

The Spinnaker Tower and Gunwharf Quays

Brief history

The Romans tramped all over these southern counties – none of the landscapes of this region could be described as grand or wild, but the countryside is consistently seductive, not least the managed woodlands of the **New Forest**. The two great maritime bases of **Portsmouth** and **Southampton** have long attracted visitors, a fair proportion of who now also pass through on their way to the more genteel pleasures of the **Isle of Wight**. You don't have to wander far off the beaten track, however, to find pretty medieval churches, manor houses, rolling landscapes and unspoilt country inns.

Spitbank Fort and the Isle of Wight ferry

Portsmouth

Britain's foremost naval station, **Portsmouth** occupies the bulbous peninsula of Portsea Island, on the eastern flank of a huge, easily defended harbour. It is a large industrialized city, its harbour clogged with naval frigates, ferries bound for the continent or the Isle of Wight, and swarms of dredgers and tugs. Due to its military importance, Portsmouth was heavily bombed during World War II, and only **Old Portsmouth**, based around the original harbour, preserves some Georgian and a little Tudor character. East of here is **Southsea**, a residential suburb of terraces with a shingle beach, seaside amusements, independent tearooms and pub-life in Albert Road reigning supreme.

Spinnaker Tower

Gunwharf Quays, PO1 3TT. ☎ 02392 857520, ⓦ spinnakertower.co.uk. Daily 10am–5.30pm. £11.95, under 15s £9.50; discounts online.

Spitbank Fort

Located between the Isle of Wight and Portsmouth, in the middle of Portsmouth Harbour, sits **Spitbank Fort**. This circular sea fort is built of granite, iron and brick and as such looks rather intimidating – it was commissioned by Lord Palmerston in 1860 as an offshore bastion. While it was intended to defend Portsmouth from French attack, it was not completed until 1878, so was not actually used in the war. There are over fifty rooms over two floors and includes a 135m-deep well.

Today, it provides more of a luxury stay, and is complete with an outdoor hot tub. Check ☎ 0330 333 7222, ⓦ solentforts.com/spitbank-fort for more information.

HMS Victory

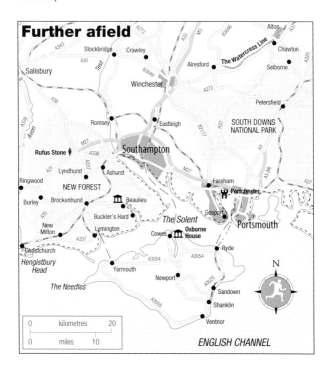

From Portsmouth Harbour train station, it's a short walk along the historic waterfront to the sleek modern **Gunwharf Quays** development, with a multitude of cafes, restaurants, nightspots and shops. Here you'll find the **Spinnaker Tower**, an elegant, 557ft-high sail-like structure, offering **views** of up to twenty miles over land and sea. Its three viewing decks can be reached by a high-speed lift, the highest one being open to the elements, though most people stick to View Deck 1, which has one of Europe's largest glass floors.

Old Portsmouth

It's a well-signposted fifteen-minute walk south of Gunwharf Quays to what remains of **Old Portsmouth**. Along the way, you pass the simple **Cathedral of St Thomas** on the High Street, whose original twelfth-century features have been obscured by rebuilding after the Civil War and again in the twentieth century. The High Street ends at a maze of cobbled Georgian streets huddling behind a fifteenth-century wall protecting the **Camber**, or old port, where Walter Raleigh landed the first potatoes and tobacco from the New World. Nearby, the Round and Square towers, which punctuate the Tudor fortifications, are popular vantage points for observing the comings and goings of the boats.

The Historic Dockyard

Victory Gate, HM Naval Base, PO1 3LJ. ① 02392 839766, ⓦ historicdockyard. co.uk. Daily 10am–5pm, varies depending on attraction. All-inclusive or 'Full Navy' ticket £39 (cheaper if bought online) excluding the Mary Rose Museum; see website for individual attraction prices. For most visitors, a trip to Portsmouth begins and ends at the **Historic Dockyard**, in the **Royal Naval Base** at the end of Queen Street. The complex comprises

three ships and several museums, with the main attractions being HMS Victory, HMS Warrior, the National Museum of the Royal Navy, the Mary Rose Museum, and a boat tour around the harbour.

HMS Warrior

Portsmouth Historic Dockyard's youngest ship, **HMS Warrior**, dates from 1860. It was Britain's first armoured (iron-clad) battleship, complete with sails and steam engines, and was the pride of the fleet in its day. The ship displays a wealth of weaponry, including rifles, pistols and sabres, though the Warrior was never challenged nor even fired a cannon in her 22 years at sea.

HMS Victory

HMS Victory was already forty years old when she set sail from Portsmouth for Trafalgar on September 14, 1805, returning in triumph three months later, but bearing the corpse of Admiral Nelson. Shot by a sniper from a French ship at the height of the

HMS Warrior

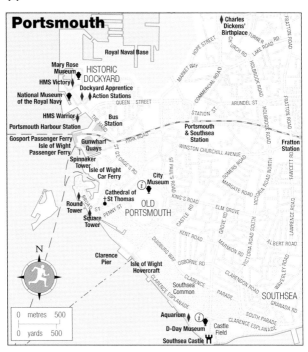

Portsmouth

- Charles Dickens' Birthplace
- Royal Naval Base
- HISTORIC DOCKYARD
- Mary Rose Museum
- HMS Victory
- Dockyard Apprentice Action Stations
- National Museum of the Royal Navy
- HMS Warrior
- Bus Station
- Portsmouth Harbour Station
- Portsmouth & Southsea Station
- Gosport Passenger Ferry
- Isle of Wight Passenger Ferry
- Gunwharf Quays
- Fratton Station
- Spinnaker Tower
- Isle of Wight Car Ferry
- City Museum
- Round Tower
- Cathedral of St Thomas
- OLD PORTSMOUTH
- Square Tower
- Clarence Pier
- Isle of Wight Hovercraft
- Southsea Common
- SOUTHSEA
- Aquarium
- D-Day Museum
- Castle Field
- Southsea Castle

HISTORIC DOCKYARD — THE HARD — QUEEN STREET — PARK ROAD — ST GEORGE'S RD — ST PAUL'S ROAD — BROAD ST — PENNY ST — KING'S ROAD — CASTLE RD — ELM GROVE — GROVE RD — KENT ROAD — MARMION RD — CLARENDON ROAD — OSBORNE RD — CLARENCE PARADE — CLARENCE ESPLANADE — SOUTHSEA ESPLANADE — SOUTH PARADE — CLARENCE ESPLANADE — GRANADA RD — WAVERLEY ROAD — ALBERT ROAD — LAWRENCE ROAD — FAWCETT RD — VICTORIA ROAD SOUTH — VICTORIA ROAD NORTH — SOMERS ROAD — MARGATE ROAD — WINSTON CHURCHILL AVENUE — STATION ST — ARUNDEL ST — FRATTON ROAD — HOLBROOK ROAD — COMMERCIAL ROAD — MARKET WAY — HOPE STREET — CHURCH RD — TURNER RD — LAKE ROAD — FRATTON ROAD — DUISBURG WAY

N

| 0 | metres | 500 |
| 0 | yards | 500 |

The Mary Rose museum

battle, Nelson succumbed to his injuries below deck three hours later, having been assured that victory was in sight. A plaque on the deck marks the spot where Nelson was fatally wounded and you can also see the wooden cask in which his body was preserved in brandy for the return trip to Britain. Although badly damaged during the battle, the Victory continued in service for a further twenty years, before being retired to the dry dock where she rests today.

National Museum of the Royal Navy

Opposite the HMS Victory, various buildings house the exhaustive **National Museum of the Royal Navy**. Tracing naval history from Alfred the Great's fleet to the present day, the collection includes some jolly figureheads, Nelson memorabilia, including the only surviving sail from HMS Victory,

Charles Dickens' Birthplace Museum

and nautical models, though coverage of more recent conflicts is scantily treated. The Trafalgar Experience is a noisy, vivid recreation of the battle itself, with gory bits to thrill the kids.

Mary Rose Museum

The impressive, boat-shaped **Mary Rose Museum** was built around Henry VIII's flagship, the **Mary Rose**, and houses not only the ship itself, but also thousands of objects retrieved from or near the wreck including guns, gold and the crew's personal effects. The ship capsized before the king's eyes off Spithead in 1545 while engaging French intruders, sinking swiftly with almost all her seven-hundred-strong crew. In 1982 a massive conservation project successfully raised the remains of the hull, which silt had preserved beneath the seabed, and you can now view the world's only remaining sixteenth-century warship through protective glass windows.

Charles Dickens' Birthplace

393 Old Commercial Rd, PO1 4QL. ☎ 02392 827261, ⓦ charlesdickensbirthplace.co.uk.

April–Sept Fri–Sun 10am–5.30pm. £4.40, under-18s free with adult.

Just over a mile northeast of Old Portsmouth, **Charles Dickens' Birthplace** is set up to look much as it would have looked when the famous novelist was born here in 1812. Charles's father, John, moved to Portsmouth in 1809 to work for the Navy Pay Office before he was recalled to London in 1815, so Charles only lived here for three years, but nevertheless he is said to have returned often and set parts of *Nicholas Nickleby* in the city. The modest house not only contains period furniture but also a wealth of information about the time when Dickens lived here, and the influences on his novels.

Southsea

Southsea boasts a wide, grassy common that looks out onto a shingle beach, where the hovercraft departs from. The Common is home to the colourful International Kite Festival, Victorious Festival and the odd car conventions throughout the calendar year. While there's a dated arcade and

The Overlord Embroidery at the D-Day Museum

fairground park lining the seafront, further inland there are plenty of tempting tavernas and bistros, independent boutique stores on Marmion Road and the ultimate, Albert Road, for its rough-n-ready pubs. This area of Portsmouth is also renowned for its vintage tearooms, quirky bric-a-brac shops and the small performance venue, the Wedgewood Rooms. During the summer, make a beeline to Southsea Bandstand, where live music/dance performances and sizzling barbeques are the main event.

Southsea Castle

Castle Esplanade, PO5 3PA. ☎ 02392 841625, ⓦ southseacastle.co.uk. Easter–Oct Tues–Sun Mon 10am–5.30pm. Free.
Next door to the D-Day Museum, Southsea's most historic building, marked by a little lighthouse, is the squat **Southsea Castle**, built from the remains of Beaulieu Abbey. You can go inside the keep and learn about Portsmouth's military history, and can climb up to the spot from where Henry VIII is said to have watched the Mary Rose sink in 1545, though in fact you can

get just as good views by climbing along the adjacent seafront ramparts. There are also free guided tunnel walks on Wednesdays and Sundays at 11am and 11.15am during the summer season.

D-Day Museum

Clarence Esplanade, PO5 3NT. ⓘ 02392 826722, ⓦ ddaymuseum.co.uk. Daily: April–Sept 10am–5.30pm; Oct–March 10am–5pm. £10, under-18s £9; discounts if booked online.
In the suburb of **Southsea**, south and west of Old Portsmouth, the **D-Day Museum** focuses on Portsmouth's role as the principal assembly point for the Normandy beach landings in World War II, code-named "Operation Overlord". It's tucked just behind Southsea Castle and near the common. There's a lot to take in here – you could easily while away two or three hours – but there's a well-thought out design route featuring exhibits, artefacts and interactive displays. Another striking exhibit is the 295ft-long Overlord Embroidery, a sort of twentieth-century equivalent of the Bayeux Tapestry, which took five years to complete.

Blue Reef Aquarium

Clarence Esplanade, PO5 3PB. ☎ 02392 875222, ⓦ bluereefaquarium.co.uk/ Portsmouth. Daily 10am–4pm, though hours can vary throughout the year; last admission at 4pm. £11.50, under 12 £8.75; discounts if booked online.

If you're looking for a rainy day option, head to the **Blue Reef Aquarium**, which is located next to the tourist office. It's home to a variety of marine life, including tropical fish, sea horses, otters, rays and sharks. There's even a walk-through underwater tunnel – try to spot the fish swimming above you. Visitors can also attend various talks and feeding sessions that are held throughout the day.

Portchester Castle

Church Rd, Portchester. Generally daily 10am–6pm. £7.90, under 17 £4.70; EH.

Six miles northwest of Portsmouth city centre, just past the marina development at Port Solent, **Portchester Castle** was built by the Romans in the third century, and boasts the finest surviving example of Roman walls in northern Europe – still over 20ft high and incorporating some twenty bastions. The Normans felt no need to make any substantial alterations when they moved in, but a keep was later built within Portchester's precincts by Henry II, which Richard II extended and Henry V used as his garrison when assembling the army that was to fight the Battle of Agincourt. Today, you can go inside the Castle or simply pack a picnic and enjoy the grassy expanses that the walls surround.

Southampton

A glance at the map gives some idea of the strategic maritime importance of **Southampton**, which stands on a triangular peninsula formed at the place where the rivers Itchen and Test flow into Southampton Water, an eight-mile inlet from the Solent. Sure enough, Southampton has figured in numerous stirring events: it witnessed the exodus of Henry V's Agincourt-bound army, the Pilgrim Fathers' departure in the

Portchester Castle

Mayflower in 1620 and the maiden voyages of such ships as the *Queen Mary* and the *Titanic*. Despite its pummelling by the Luftwaffe and some disastrous postwar urban sprawl, the thousand-year-old city has retained some of its medieval charm in parts and reinvented itself as a twenty-first century shopping centre in others, with the giant glass-and-steel West Quay as its focus. A short stroll north of here, Southampton's impressive Cultural Quarter is worth a visit, with its open squares, excellent art gallery and the superb Sea City Museum.

City Art Gallery

Civic Centre, Commercial Rd. ☎ 023 8083 3000, 🌐 southamptonartgallery.com. Mon–Fri 10am–3pm, Sat 10am–5pm. Free.

Core of the modern town is the Civic Centre, a short walk east of the train station and home to the excellent **Southampton City Art Gallery**, which originally opened in 1939. Its collection is particularly strong on contemporary British artists with works by Gilbert and George, Anthony Gormley and Andy Goldsworthy. Older paintings are also on show, among them works by Gainsborough, Joshua Reynolds and the Impressionists – Monet and Pissarro included.

The Sea City Museum

Civic Centre, Havelock Rd. ☎ 023 8083 3007, 🌐 seacitymuseum.co.uk. Daily 10am–5pm. £8.50, under 16s and over 60s £6.

The purpose-built **Sea City Museum** is a triumph of design that succeeds in being both

The West Quay shopping centre and medieval walls in Southampton

moving and fun. Opened on April 10, 2012, the hundredth anniversary of the day that the Titanic sailed from Southampton's Town Quay on its maiden voyage, the museum provides a fascinating insight into the history of the ship, its crew, its significance to Edwardian Southampton and, of course, an account of the fateful journey, which started in high excitement to end only four days later in tragedy.

Lymington and around

Lying between Southampton and Bournemouth, the most pleasant point of access for ferries to the Isle of Wight is **Lymington**, a sheltered haven that's become one of the busiest leisure harbours on the south coast. Rising from the quay area, the cobbled street of the old town is lined with Georgian houses. At the top of the High Street (opposite Church Lane) is the partly thirteenth century church of **St Thomas the Apostle**, with a cupola-topped tower built in 1670.

The New Forest

Covering about 220 square miles, the **New Forest** is one of southern England's favourite rural playgrounds. The New Forest enjoys a unique patchwork of ancient laws and privileges alongside the regulations applying

Stream in the New Forest

to its National Park status. The **trees** here are now much more varied than they were in pre-Norman times, with birch, holly, yew, Scots pine and other conifers interspersed with the ancient oaks and beeches. The most conspicuous species of **fauna** is the New Forest **pony** – you'll see them grazing nonchalantly by the roadsides and ambling through some villages. The local deer are less visible now that some of the faster roads are fenced, although several species still roam the woods, including the tiny **sika deer**, descendants of a pair that escaped from nearby Beaulieu in 1904.

Camping in the New Forest

There are ten campsites throughout the Forest run by Camping in the Forest (☎ 0845 130 8224, ⦿ campingintheforest.co.uk); all are open from mid-April to early Sept, and some are open year-round. Some are very simple, with few or no facilities, others have electricity and hot shower blocks, but they all have open access to the Forest, many have streams and fords running through them, with ponies and donkeys wandering freely.

ACCOMMODATION

Luccombe Hall Hotel

Accommodation

There's a great range of accommodation available on the Isle of Wight, from generous self-catering options to humble campsites and converted guesthouses to cosy B&Bs. Camping is another popular way to stay on the island (weather permitting). There are plenty of campsites spread across the island, many set in picturesque settings, and is a great base to explore more of the island from. Alternatively, if you're looking for a little more privacy or for the ultimate home-away-from-home feel, there's a wide array of self-catering accommodation, from short- to long-stay. The prices we quote for hotels, guesthouses and B&Bs in this Guide generally refer to the cheapest available double room in high season (usually August), including breakfast, unless otherwise stated. There are just two YHA hostels on the island – one in Brighstone and one in Totland – visit ⓦ www.yha.org.uk/ places-to-stay/isle-of-wight to book your stay. Some hotels offer discounted ferry and public transport passes. Note that rates rise considerably during Cowes Week (late July/early August) so book well in advance, but there are lower rates and usually much more choice during the off-season.

Cowes and around

ALBERT COTTAGE MAP P.28. York Ave, East Cowes, PO32 6BD. ⓣ 01983 299309, ⓦ albertcottagehotel.com. Once part of Victoria and Albert's Osborne Estate, this Grade II-listed building is now a boutique hotel offering ten bedrooms. Set amongst picturesque acres of gardens, Albert Cottage retains a Victorian country-house ambience, with cream-coloured and wooden furniture across their double and twin rooms and suites. Also on-site is their slick *Consort Restaurant*. **£145**

BUSIGNY HOUSE MAP P.30. 16 Castle Rd, West Cowes, PO31 7QZ. ⓣ 01983 291919, ⓦ www.quaymanagement.co.uk/ accommodation/busigny-house. This spacious guesthouse spans three floors and sleeps up to 18 guests: you can either rent by the room (eight in total) or the entire house itself. The attention to detail – mostly coastal-themed, of course – makes it a home away from home and is in an enviable location, just 5min from the Marina and Northwood Park. From **£100**

THE CALEDON MAP P.28. 59 Mill Hill Rd, West Cowes, PO31 7EG. ⓣ 01983 293599, ⓦ the-caledon.co.uk. Slick, stylish guesthouse, with rooms offering sea views. The rooms (all en suite) include basic amenities, the lounge has a small honesty bar and breakfasts taken in the breakfast room can be modified to your liking. It's in a convenient spot, right outside the bus stop to/from Newport, and is a 5min walk downhill to the Floating Bridge across to East Cowes. **£119**

DUKE OF YORK MAP P.30. Mill Hill Rd, PO31 7BT. ⓣ 01983 195171, ⓦ www. dukeofyorkcowes.co.uk. This B&B is just around the corner from the crossing to East

Cowes and the lively high street, and is a pub in itself as well. All rooms are en suite and include a full English breakfast in the price. Rooms are a modern, basic style and has a relaxed atmosphere. **£79**

HOLLY TREE HOUSE MAP P.28. 218 Park Rd, PO31 7NG. ☎ 01983 246227, ⓦ www.hollytreehousecowes.co.uk. Rooms are available to rent by the night or week at this stylishly spartan B&B, with coastal furnishings and comfy beds. There are four rooms to choose from, each named after a different area of the island, and are individually styled. **£85**

INTO THE WOODS MAP P.28. Lower Westwood, Brocks Copse Rd, Wootton, PO33 4NP ☎ 07769 696464, ⓦ isleofwighttreehouse.com. Two luxury tree houses (one sleeps up to six, the other two) and a hideaway consisting of four exclusive huts (sleeps up to six) in Wootton, around three miles south of East Cowes. This is perfect for a spot of rugged glamping; think woodburners, en-suite showers and hot tubs. All self-catering, you'll feel right at the heart of nature in this peaceful setting, with plenty of space in the woods for kids to run around. Two-night minimum. **£150**

THE LITTLE GLOSTER MAP P.28. 31 Marsh Rd, Gurnard Marsh, PO31 8JQ ☎ 01983 200299, ⓦ thelittlegloster.com. In Gurnard, west of Cowes, sits *The Little Gloster*, a Scandinavian-styled hotel-restaurant right on the water's edge. You can choose to stay in one of three stylish guest rooms that each have their own unique selling point – duplex windows, a balcony, private sitting room – and all overlook the sea. **£130**

NEW HOLMWOOD HOTEL MAP P.28. 65 Queen's Rd, PO31 8BW. ☎ 01983 292508, ⓦ www.newholmwoodhotel.co.uk. This spacious hotel features 26 rooms, some with sea views, and suites include a lounge. Rooms can be adapted into twin or double rooms as necessary. There's also a restaurant, with a patio looking out towards the cruise ships and freight ships passing by. **£127**

NORTH HOUSE MAP P.30. 32 Sun Hill, PO31 7TP. ☎ 01983 209453, ⓦ northhousecowes.co.uk. This spacious hotel is set in a lovely building that backs out onto itself, in a relaxed setting perfect for recharging the batteries. There's a heated swimming pool in the summer, a terraced garden and inside is a fine-dining restaurant, stylish bar and chic reading room. Each room is individually styled in an understated fashion, with rolltop bathtubs, luxury toiletries and friendly staff to hand. A stay here is highly recommended. **£195**

UNION INN MAP P.30. Watch House Lane, West Cowes, PO31 7QH ☎ 01983 293163, ⓦ unioninncowes.co.uk. Above their popular historic pub are six small rooms at the *Union Inn*. The rooms (all en-suite) are individually styled and feature one wall of printed wallpaper. What they lack in space they make up for in location: not only are you just off the high street but you're right in the heart of the action for Cowes Week, and there's a busy bar downstairs. Rate includes breakfast. **£90**

VILLA ROTHSAY MAP P.28. 29 Baring Rd, West Cowes, PO31 8DF ☎ 01983 295178, ⓦ villa-rothsay.co.uk. Named after King Edward VII (Queen Victoria's eldest son), who was the Duke of Rothesay when he regularly visited the Villa at the time. The likes of the drawing room and the staircase make you feel like you've been transported back to the Victorian age with its traditional decor, but the bedrooms are slightly more up to date with televisions, hot drinks facilities and modern bathrooms (including light-ringed mirrors). You can't beat the views, either; wave to the passing yachts from the balcony. Their library and garden terrace are perfect for relaxing with a book and soaking up the rays. **£155**

Newport and around

CALVERTS MAP P.38. 27 Quay St, PO30 5BA ☎ 01983 525281, ⓦ www.calvertshotel.co.uk. This grade II-listed building was once home to the mayor, but today functions as a budget hotel with plenty of character. The rooms are pretty basic, which can be expected at the rates, but are all en suite and include a television and other basic amenities. They also have a bar, breakfast room and a large lounge. **£28**

Best campsites

Nodes Point Holiday Park; see page 105
Appuldurcombe Gardens Holiday Park; see page 106
Compton Farm; see page 106
Calborne Water Mill; see page 107
The Orchards Holiday Park; see page 107

HEWITT'S HOUSE MAP P.38. 33 Lugley St, PO30 5ET. ☏ 01983 822994, ⓦ https://www.hewittshouse.com. Six spacious rooms with wooden furnishings, desk space, a fine-dining restaurant, pleasant gardens, a breakfast room and after-dinner lounge. All are en suite and offer a shower and bath, with rooms located at the front of the building or overlooking the gardens. **£59**

ONE HOLYROOD B&B MAP P.38. 1 Holyrood St, PO30 5AU ☏ 01983 521717, ⓦ oneholyrood.co.uk. Twelve spacious rooms and one self-contained apartment available at this B&B, with discounted Red Funnel and Wightlink journeys if you book your stay with them. Aside from its Grade II-listed status, guests can enjoy a tearoom, and secluded terrace and garden that are filled with scented plants all year round. **£50**

WHEATSHEAF MAP P.38. 16 St Thomas' Square, PO30 1SG. ☏ 01983 532444, ⓦ www.thewheatsheafhotel.com. Attractively located by a string of cafés, shops and overlooking St Thomas' Square, this hotel features bright, airy rooms – think white panelling and furniture, rolltop bathtubs, faux-fur throws – and it is also home to a popular tearoom and brasserie restaurant, with mains from £10.95. **£59**

Ryde and around

ROYAL ESPLANADE MAP P.46. 16 Esplanade, PO33 2ED. ☏ 01983 562549, ⓦ www.royalesplanadehotel.co.uk. Undoubtedly the best location in Ryde, with some rooms overlooking the hovercraft terminal and situated in a grand, Victorian building along the Esplanade: there's no missing it. Rooms can be spacious and have a mixture of modern and old-fashioned stylings. The owners are friendly and the restaurant and breakfast room offer sea views, and there's also a bar. **£50**

RYDE CASTLE MAP P.46. The Esplanade, PO33 1JA ☏ 08456 086040, ⓦ oldenglishinns.co.uk. The popular Ryde Castle sits just behind the Ryde Esplanade and is a great place to retreat to after a day at the beach – even if you just want a drink at their beach-facing pub-garden. There are 11 rooms to choose from which are well decorated with modern stylings in a traditional setting: think log fires, wooden staircases and overall warm hues. **£170**

SORRENTO LODGE MAP P.46. 11 The Strand, PO33 2LG ☏ 01983 812813, ⓦ sorrentolodge.co.uk. This is a perfect seaside spot, pleasantly tucked away from the main action but still within walking distance of it all. The B&B is housed in a Grade II-listed building and houses three double rooms, two double/twin rooms and two family-sized suites. Discounts available if you stay more than one night. **£80**

YELF'S MAP P.46. 54 Union St, PO33 2LG. ☏ 01983 564062, ⓦ www.yelfshotel.com. With a warm charm and atmosphere, *Yelf's* was one of the island's original coaching inns, and now offers 40 rooms. All are en suite with basic amenities and is in a handy spot on Union St. Rooms are decent enough, with basic furnishings. **£75**

The east coast

ARIA RESORTS PRIORY BAY HOTEL MAP P.50. Priory Drive, near Seaview, PO33 1YA ☏ 01983 613146, ⓦ priorybay.com. At the time of writing, this upmarket hotel was undergoing extensive redevelopment and should have reopened into an even snazzier spot by the time you're reading this. Set in sixty acres of ground, guests will have access to a secluded beach, swimming pool, bar and a restaurant.

NODES POINT HOLIDAY PARK MAP P.50. Nodes Rd, St Helens, PO33 1YA ☎ 01983 872401, Ⓦ www.parkdeanresorts.co.uk/location/isle-of-wight/nodes-point. You can either bring your own caravans and tents or hire them here at this holiday park, which boasts an excellent position in Bembridge overlooking the bay. The facilities are excellent, with a sports court, indoor heated pool (with a waterslide) and an adventure playground, as well as a bar restaurant. Just remember to pull yourself away to check out the rest of Bembridge! Caravans two-night stay minimum. **£328**

NORTHBANK HOTEL MAP P.50. Circular Rd, PO34 5ET ☎ 01983 612227, Ⓦ northbankhotel.co.uk. This white-walled boutique hotel runs down to the beach via its small sloped garden, with superlative views across the Solent. Offering 18 rooms – most of which have a seaview – the rooms are a mix of traditional and modern, with nautical details peppered throughout. You can take breakfast or dinner here, with a menu using locally sourced produce and a rather tempting wine list. **£100**

PILOT BOAT INN MAP P.50. Station Rd, Bembridge, PO35 5NN ☎ 01983 872077, Ⓦ thepilotboatinn.com. There's no missing the *Pilot Boat Inn*, with its ground floor exterior styled like the blue hull of a boat – portholes and all. Inside, there are five rooms (all en suite) to choose from and all available at the same rates. With wash stations, eBike charging points and secure bicycle storage, it's a good option for cyclists and walkers. **£80**

THE SEAVIEW MAP P.50. The High St, PO34 5EX ☎ 01983 612711, Ⓦ seaviewhotel.co.uk. Slap bang in the middle of Seaview is this grandiose, ivy-clad Victorian townhouse. The 18 rooms vary in size and some offer sea views, but all are comfortable and the gardens run down to the beach. It's good for families and has a daily-changing menu, all homecooked and using local produce. **£100**

The south coast
AQUA HOTEL MAP P.58. 17 The Esplanade, PO37 6BN ☎ 01983 863024,

Ⓦ theaqua.co.uk. Like a square chunk of chalk jutting out from the cliffside, this family-run hotel along the Shanklin Esplanade has its own brasserie restaurant (breakfast and dinner) and a sea-facing terrace out at the front. Some of the bright, modern-furnished rooms (all en suite) have their own balconies overlooking the sea. There is also an entertainment lounge and separate bar area. Sea-view double rooms **£108**, rear-view double rooms **£90**

THE BELMORE MAP P.58. 101 Station Ave, PO36 8HD ☎ 01983 404189, Ⓦ www.facebook.com/thebelmoreguesthouse. A boutique B&B with calming, coastal colour schemes – think pastel greens, deep-sea blues and ocean-spray whites – just off the northern end of Sandown Esplanade. The spacious rooms are all en-suite and are styled with the likes of porthole mirrors, yacht-printed cushions and gloss-tiled bathrooms. **£76**

THE HAVELOCK MAP P.58. 2 Queen's Rd, PO37 6AN ☎ 01983 862747, Ⓦ havelockhotel.co.uk. A range of 22 stylish, modern rooms here at this clifftop hotel, which also boasts a Mediterranean-esque outdoor pool (heated), well-clipped gardens and free parking. Rates include breakfast, and some rooms have balconies. Three-night minimum stay. **£240**

LUCCOMBE HALL MAP P.58. Luccombe Rd, PO37 6RL ☎ 01983 869000, Ⓦ luccombehall.co.uk. This sprawling country house, set amongst four acres of gardens, has amazing views from its clifftop position down over Shanklin beach and the Solent beyond, which you can admire from its gardens, windowed terrace or (some) rooms. There are 29 rooms in total: choose from standard, sea-facing, family or even one with its own private hot tub, among other room types. Facilities include indoor and outdoor children's play areas, heated swimming pools, games room and even a mini putting green. **£180**

RYLSTONE MANOR MAP P.58. Rylstone Gardens, PO37 6RG ☎ 01983 862806, Ⓦ rylstone-manor.co.uk. Each room is named after a different tree, and as such are individually styled while retaining the overall style of this Victorian house. That's not the only thing that makes it a quaint place to stay, though, as it's nestled in the heart of the leafy Rylstone Gardens. **£72.50**

Ventnor to Blackgang

APPULDURCOMBE GARDENS HOLIDAY PARK MAP P.66. Wroxall, PO38 3EP ☎ 01983 852597, Ⓦ appuldurcombegardens.co.uk. This award-winning holiday park is set amongst 14 acres of secluded grounds with the open countryside beyond – and just three miles from Shanklin and Ventnor. Part of the island's Area of Outstanding Natural Beauty, this is a fab spot for those looking for walks, cycles and birdwatching; as for the campsite itself, the on-site facilities can complement your stay. There's a range of accommodation options, including lodges, motorhomes, static camping and apartments; these rates vary, and also depend on the time of year you're visiting – check the website for individual rates.

ENCHANTED MANOR MAP P.66. Sandrock Rd, PO38 2NG ☎ 01983 730215, Ⓦ enchantedmanor.co.uk. Fairy-themed guesthouse in Niton with extravagant rooms that sleeps up to 22 guests, and features fairy-tale artworks. It's certainly a unique spot for a romantic stay; there's also a billiard room, games room and bar.

THE HAMBROUGH MAP P.66. Hambrough Rd, Ventnor, PO38 1SQ ☎ 01938 856333, Ⓦ thehambrough.com. Seven slick, simple rooms all with seaviews (bar one) spread across two floors. A great place to relax, unwind and take part in nearby coastal activities, from walks and sailing to horse-riding and sunbathing. They also run three self-catering properties: Quince Cottage, Villa Lavinia and Villa Apartment – check their website for further details. **£150**

THE LECONFIELD MAP P.66. 85 Leeson Rd, Upper Bonchurch, PO38 1PU, Ⓦ leconfieldhotel.com. Beautifully decorated and luxurious hotel. They offer discounted car ferry travel (Southampton, Lymington or Portsmouth) and provide free bus travel. The swish rooms are named after maritime themes – there's

the Mermaid, Seahorse and Nemo rooms amongst others – and are all en-suite. No children (under 18s) or pets permitted. Around the house, you can enjoy amazing seaviews from the conservatory, stylish sitting rooms to make any captain proud and helpful owners ready to assist you with making the most of this scenic area. **£110**

ROYAL HOTEL MAP P.66. Belgrave Rd, Ventnor, PO38 1JJ ☎ 01938 852186, Ⓦ royalhoteliow.co.uk. The clue is in the name with this sprawling 52-bedroomed complex, one of the island's oldest hotels built in 1832. The hotel is far from stuck in the past, with elegantly styled rooms mixing classic and contemporary in just the right amounts. Make sure you enjoy breakfast in the conservatory or dinner in the plush restaurant. **£225**

ST AUGUSTINE VILLA MAP P.66. Esplanade, Ventnor, PO38 1TA ☎ 01983 852285, Ⓦ harbourviewhotel.co.uk. This blue-plaque Victorian mansion sits halfway down the winding road to Ventnor Esplanade, and is one of the more scenic buildings here. The rooms all offer seaviews (some have limited views) and while they don't offer any meals, they're in close proximity to award-winning restaurants such as the *Smoking Lobster*. **£86**

Brighstone to Alum Bay

COMPTON FARM MAP P.76. Brook, PO30 4HF ☎ 01983 740215, Ⓦ comptonfarm. co.uk. This basic campsite is set on a level field surrounded by an 18-acre wildflower meadow, and is within easy walking distance from the beach. Showers cost extra but all other facilities are included (toilets, laundry room, washing up stations). Open Easter–Oct. Pitch **£20**

FARRINGFORD MAP P.76. Bedbury Lane, Freshwater Bay, PO40 9PE. ☎ 01983 752500, Ⓦ farringford.co.uk/self-catering-isle-of-wight/holiday-cottages. Choose from one of five self-catering cottages – most sleep two or four guests but a couple sleep up to seven. The Alfred Cottages are charmingly cute with blue-panelled exterior, high ceilings and fitted woodburners (logs provided), while the bricked Stable Cottages span two floors and include their own courtyard. **£210**

GRANGE FARM MAP P.76. Military Rd, PO30 4DA ⓣ 01983 740296, ⓦ grangefarmholidays.com. Choose from campsites (traditional to electrical hook-ups), static caravans or cottages here at this family-run farm, spread across 60 acres of land. Overlooking Brighstone Bay, the site also includes a playground, a facilities block (free showers, washing machines, baby-changing areas) and a reception-shop for food essentials (including the most essential item of all: ice cream). **£21**

TOM'S ECO LODGE MAP P.76. Tapnell Farm, Newport Rd, PO41 0YJ ⓣ 07717 666346, ⓦ tomsecolodge.com. There's a range of quirky glamping options here, from tents and cabins to pods, domes and modulogs (cabins designed exclusively for *Tom's Eco Lodge*). They can all be rented on Tapnell Farm, an area that offers privacy and seaviews all rolled into one. Ecopods **£163**

Yarmouth and around

THE BUGLE COACHING INN MAP P.87. The Square, PO41 0NS ⓣ 01983 760272, ⓦ www.characterinns.co.uk/the-bugle-coaching-inn. This sixteenth-century coaching inn is best known for its hearty grub, but that should be good enough reason to stay over as well, right? Upstairs are seven en-suite rooms, some with views overlooking the Market Square, with plain walls, wooden furniture and blue decor. Rates include breakfast. **£70**

CALBORNE WATER MILL MAP P.84. Westover, Calbourne, PO30 4JN ⓣ 01983 531227, ⓦ calbournewatermill.co.uk. Within the mill complex, you can take your pick from luxury eco-friendly lodges, traditional cottages and a camping and caravan park. As well as being close to a fenced stream, roaming peacocks and overlooking the peaceful woodland, there's also a café on site that serves up delicious Sunday lunches. Tents/caravans/campervans per pitch **£10**

THE GEORGE HOTEL MAP P.87. Quay St, PO41 0PE ⓣ 01983 760331, ⓦ thegeorge.co.uk. This seventeenth-century townhouse, squeezed in between Yarmouth Castle and the pier, sits on the water's edge and isn't far from the ferry terminal. The rooms are lavishly decorated to the perfect amount, and there's a fantastic restaurant on site. And why not give their morning yoga class a go? **£225**

JIREH HOUSE MAP P.87. St James' Square, PO41 0NP ⓣ 01983 760513, ⓦ www.jireh-house.com. This quaint, seventeenth-century cottage is a cosy fit of seven rooms, three of which share bathroom facilities. It retains a traditional character throughout, and rooms include a small television and hot drinks facilities. There's a popular teahouse downstairs, where guests can enjoy breakfast from, and is usually bustling all afternoon until close. **£90**

THE ORCHARDS HOLIDAY PARK MAP P.84. Main Rd, Newbridge, PO41 0TS ⓣ 01983 531331, ⓦ orchards-holiday-park.co.uk. Just over four miles southeast of Yarmouth is this family-owned holiday park, with a range of accommodation types available, from tent pitches and caravans to hiring your own static caravan. You can also rent out their stone-built Orchard House, which is just next to the park and with its own garden. Amenities include a coffee shop, indoor and outdoor pools, table tennis and more. Three-night minimum stay and decent package and non-package deals (ie including return ferry). Prices vary; check website.

ESSENTIALS

Cycling in Sandown

Arrival

Make your entrance to the Isle of Wight from a choice of ferries, catamarans or hovercraft. Whichever way you choose, as you approach the island across the Solent (the strait between the mainland and the island), you'll pass by plenty of sailing yachts and speedboats zigzagging across the waves also en route to the island or further afield. From London, it takes around three hours by car or just over two and a half hours by public transport, with three well-connected mainland points (Portsmouth, Southampton and Lymington) to make the final leg of the journey across from.

By ferry

There are three departure points from the mainland: Portsmouth, Southampton and Lymington. Fare structures and schedules on all routes are labyrinthine, so check the companies' websites for full details of current fares and schedules.

From **Portsmouth**, Wightlink runs car ferries from the Gunwharf Terminal to Fishbourne (daily 1–2 hourly, 3am–11.59pm; 45min), and a high-speed catamaran from the Harbour to Ryde Pier (foot passengers only; 5.15am–10.45pm; every 25min at peak times; hourly at quieter times; 22min).

Lymington to Yarmouth offers the fastest car ferry route (40min) with Wightlink car ferries (☎03339 997333, ⓦwightlink.co.uk).

Red Funnel operates a high-speed catamaran from **Southampton** to West Cowes (foot passengers only; Mon–Sat 3am–11.59pm, Sun 3am–10pm; every hour; 25min) and one with cars to East Cowes (similar hours; 55min). You can jump on the free shuttle bus service from Southampton Central train station to the ferry terminal.

These timetables may vary slightly by season; check the relevant websites for details.

By hovercraft

Hovertravel (☎01983 717700, ⓦhovertravel.co.uk) runs hovercrafts from Clarence Esplanade in Southsea to Ryde (foot passengers only; every 30min Mon–Fri 6.30am–8pm, Sat 8am–10pm, Sun 9am–9pm; 10min). This is certainly the most unique way to reach the island, being the world's only commercial passenger hovercraft service. Bumping along the waves on one of these 'flights' is a unique way to make your entrance to the island, and you can take light luggage on board with you. The hovercraft pulls up along the Esplanade, next to the bus station, but note the timetable can be affected when there are adverse weather conditions.

By air

There are two small airfields on the Isle of Wight, in Bembridge (ⓦeghj. extremelynice.net/eghj) and Sandown (ⓦeghn.org.uk), but these are for private

Travelling to the Isle of Wight

Lymington to Yarmouth: Wightlink ☎03339 997333, ⓦwightlink. co.uk.
Portsmouth to Fishbourne or Ryde Pier: Wightlink ☎03339 997333, ⓦwightlink.co.uk.
Southampton to Cowes: Red Funnel ☎02380 019192, ⓦredfunnel.co.uk
Southsea to Ryde: Hovertravel ☎01983 717700, ⓦhovertravel.co.uk

planes only. If you're coming from further afield, you'll need to fly into one of the mainland airports and make your way down by car or train to one of the ferry ports listed in this chapter.

By public transport

Visitors can buy an all-in-one ticket from National Express (☎ 08717 818181, ⊕ nationalexpress.com), which covers a coach from a range of cities to Southsea, boarding the hovercraft to Ryde. Prices vary depending on your starting location and tends to be cheaper if booked in advance, but a ticket from London Victoria Coach Station to Ryde costs around £25 for a return journey.

Getting around

With efficient and (mostly) modern public transport available, it's easy enough to get around the island without a car. Buses are fairly frequent and there are free timetables you can pick up at stations and visitor information points, which detail bus and train routes and timetables. There aren't any motorways on the Isle of Wight, just country roads and main roads, but everywhere is well signposted and easy to navigate, making it an ideal destination for keen walkers and cyclists.

Buses

Local buses are run by Southern Vectis (☎ 01983 827000, ⊕ islandbuses.info), who sell good-value tickets offering unlimited travel across their network. The buses are bright green, single- and double-decker and are modern, including USB charging points. For unlimited bus travel for 24 hours, opt for Day Rover tickets (adults £10, ages 5–16 £5, groups up to five £25), while Rover+Breezer tickets are available for 24 or 48 hour travel (£12/£16, ages 17–18 £9/£12, ages 5–16 £6/£8, groups up to five £30/£37.50). Weekly Freedom tickets are good value for longer stays (7 days for £25, ages 17–18 £20, ages 5–16 £13.50, groups up to five £60).

Tickets can be bought via their mobile app, their Travel Shops or direct from the driver. Some hotels even offer free or discounted bus passes for guests.

Bus routes

Bus #1 Newport to Cowes; bus #2 Newport to Ryde via Merstone; bus #3 Newport to Ryde via Rookley; bus #4 Ryde to East Cowes; bus #5 Newport to East Cowes; bus #6 Newport to Ventnor; bus #7 Newport to Totland;

Take a day out on a bus tour

Southern Vectis run four hop-on, hop-off bus tours during the summer season. These open-top tourist buses run daily and include commentaries about the sights and attractions you pass by. See below for individual routes and operating months.

The **Downs Breezer** runs between Ryde and Seaview via Quarr Abbey, Wootton Station, Dinosaur Isle and Bembridge (daily May–Sept); the **Island Coaster** runs between Ryde and Yarmouth via Shanklin, Ventnor and Blackgang Chine (daily April–Sept); the **Needles Breezer** runs between Yarmouth and Needles Battery (daily mid-March to Sept); and the **Shanklin Shuttle** covers the Chine, Old Village, main town and beachfront Esplanade (daily May–Sept).

bus #8 Newport to Ryde via Amazon World and Bembridge; bus #9 Newport to Ryde via Wootton; bus #12 Newport to Totland; bus #22 Shanklin to Lake & Sibden Hill; bus #24 Yaverland to Shanklin; bus #32 Cowes to Northwood circular via Gurnard.

Most run half-hourly or hourly; check the website for individual and up-to-date timetables.

Trains

There are two rail lines on the island. The Island Line (every 20–40min; ⓦ southwesternrailway.com) spans 8.5-miles and runs from Ryde Pier to Smallbrook Junction (10min), Brading (15min), Sandown (20min), Lake (21min) and Shanklin (25min). Rather uniquely, they are made up of former London Underground carriages; a huge 2019 investment will include new rolling stock and is expected to

improve cross-Solent connectivity as well as renewing the Ryde Railway Pier, all of which is due to be completed and fully operational by 2021.

The second rail line is the five-mile Isle of Wight Steam Railway (ⓦ iwsteamrailway.co.uk) which runs from Wootton to Smallbrook Junction (6–9 daily, 30min) where it connects with the Island Line.

Cycling

Cycling is a popular way of getting around the island; ferries, catamarans and the hovercraft all accept bikes on board. There's the 65-mile Round the Island route, which is well-signposted (white signs with a blue island means clockwise, blue signs with a white island anti-clockwise). In the summer, the narrow lanes can get very busy, but stopping off at small towns along the way helps break the journey up.

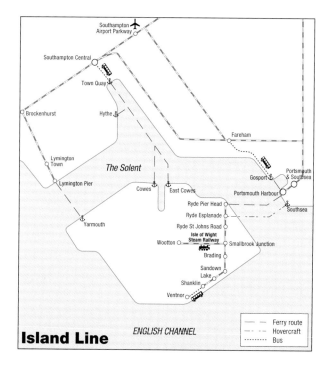

Island Line

If you're looking to rent a bike, there are plenty of options. Check out Wight Cycle Hire in Yarmouth (£12/half-day, £16/day; ☎ 01983 761800, 🖥 wightcyclehire.co.uk); Isle Cycle in Sandown (£15/day, £70/week; ☎ 01983 400055, 🖥 islecycle.co.uk); Two Elements in Cowes (mountain bike four hours £15; ☎ 07947912886, 🖥 twoelements.co.uk); and Routetfifty7 in Shanklin (£13/half-day, £18/day; ☎ 01983 875542, 🖥 routefifty7.com), amongst many more. Most of these have multi-day options and they can collect and deliver bikes across the island. Ebikes are also readily available.

Some would argue that cycling is the best way to experience the Isle of Wight: routes will see you take in a variety of landscapes, from fantastic stretches of coastline and narrow country roads to dense woodland and pretty estuaries.

Walking
The majority of the island is a designated Area of Outstanding Natural Beauty and is a very popular destination for walkers and hikers, with a variety of gradients to choose from. The coastal, public footpath around the island covers roughly 68 miles, which experienced walkers could complete in as little as four days, although this is one of the more challenging options. There are various walking guides available in bookstores such as *Medina* in Cowes (see page 32), and plenty of resources online, too.

The island is quite hilly, which is something to bear in mind if you're trying to track down a hotel with a suitcase in tow, and huge buses weave through steep, narrow roads, so always mind where you're going. It's important to wear appropriate footwear, particularly if you're covering some of the hilly headlands, and for some parts it may even be useful to use a pair of Nordic walking poles.

Driving
Although driving is the most straightforward way to get around the island, the Isle of Wight supports a number of local sustainability schemes to encourage drivers to leave your car at home. This is within reason, of course, and there are still many conveniently placed car parks dotted around the island. Some hotels provide free parking to guests, a few sights offer discounted entry to visitors who have reached them by 'sustainable methods' (by foot, bike or public transport) and there are five electric car charge points for electric vehicles.

That said, the absence of motorways on the island means that there are some lovely, scenic routes past large stretches of countryside and horizon-lined coastal views: worth navigating are Middle Road from Newport to Freshwater, and Military Road from Freshwater to Chale.

To find out more about renting a car on the island, head to 🖥 visitisleofwight.co.uk/travel/getting-around/by-car.

Boat trips
Flanked by the Solent and English Channel, guided boat trips and pleasure cruises are a great way to take in the surroundings of the island by water. Needles Pleasure Cruises offer 'slow' and 'fast' cruises from five various-sized boats (☎ 01983 761587, 🖥 www.needlespleasurecruises.co.uk/the-trips); board at the end of the jetty on Alum Bay. Trips vary in length of time depending on the tide and type of boat, with routes covering Yarmouth, The Needles and Scratchell's Bay.

There's also **Coral Star** (☎ 01983 760212, 🖥 www.coralstar.co.uk), a blue, wooden boat providing running commentaries between routes from Yarmouth to the Needles, and even across to Lymington on the mainland (Saturdays only).

Directory A–Z

Children

The island is great fun for children of all ages, with long stretches of beaches, themed amusement parks and plenty of watersports to get stuck into.

Most pubs and restaurants are family-friendly, and some have family rooms or beer gardens where children are welcome. While plenty offer family rooms, some B&Bs and hotels don't accept children under a certain age (usually 12), but there's plenty of self-catering accommodation for however many are in your group – it can be easier (and more fun) for kids, too.

Many public museums and attractions have kids' activity packs, family events, play areas and more, and you can find a playground or park in most neighbourhoods. Children (usually under 16s) are usually entitled to concessionary rates across many attractions, and under-5s generally travel free on public transport.

Cinema

There are just two cinemas on the Isle of Wight: a Cineworld in Newport (Coppins Bridge, PO30 2TA; Ⓦ www.cineworld.co.uk/cinemas/newport-isle-of-wight) and Commodore in Ryde (2 Star St, PO33 2HX; Ⓦ leoleisurecommodore.co.uk/ryde/now). Both are multi-screened and show the latest blockbusters.

Over the summer months, a range of outdoor cinema screenings take place across some lovely locations, such as **Puckpool Park** in Seaview, **Mottistone Gardens** in Newport and **Ventnor Botanic Gardens**. **The Garlic Farm** (see page 39) screens cult classics and family-friendly films (usually over the Bank Holiday weekends) on-site where guests can tuck into barbecue food and purchase hot and cold drinks from the restaurant; tickets are usually around £8.

There's also the **Isle of Wight Film Festival**, part of the **Ventnor Fringe Festival** (see page 65), which screens classic and independent films throughout the year – check out Ⓦ vfringe.co.uk for more information.

Crime and emergencies

The Isle of Wight does not see a lot of crime and visitors will feel safe in most areas, but as with most places, it's still important to act sensibly and report anything that doesn't look right.

The emergency numbers for the Police, Fire Brigade, Ambulance and Coastguard are ☏ 999, or ☏ 111 for non-emergencies.

Discount passes

Many of the island's historic attractions – from castles to stately homes – are owned and/or operated by either the National Trust (Ⓦ nationaltrust.org.uk; denoted as NT in the Guide) and English Heritage (Ⓦ english-heritage.org.uk; EH). They usually charge entry fees, though some sites are free for members.

A few hotels on the island offer free bus passes, while other hotels provide discounts for island-crossing travel if you book directly with them. There are a range of combination-package deals (ie transport and accommodation) covered in one price, which can be worth taking advantage of depending on the length of the trip or simply to save you some time.

More and more attractions are beginning to offer discounted entry if you arrive to their site by sustainable transport (walking, cycling or public transport).

Electricity

The current is 240V AC. North American appliances will need a transformer and adaptor; those from Europe, South Africa, Australia and New Zealand only need an adaptor.

Health
There is one hospital on the Isle of Wight, in Newport (St Mary's Hospital Parkhurst Rd, PO30 5TG; ☎ 01983 524081, ⊚ iow.nhs.uk). There are medical centres and pharmacies across the island, in both main towns and surrounding areas. The Isle of Wight NHS website provides an extensive list of every pharmacy on the island including their address, website and telephone number (☎ 01983 524081, ⊚ www.iow.nhs.uk).

Internet
Free wi-fi is available in most places, although the speed varies depending where you are – you're less likely to have a strong connection on Tennyson Down compared to Newport's high street, for instance. Some of the older hotels and sights out in the sticks might not have fast connections as their number one priority. It's best to take printed copies of timetables and maps with you – and this guidebook, of course – where you don't need to rely on signal to navigate your way around, particularly if you're cycling or hiking.

Left luggage
There aren't any official luggage storage points on the island, nor can you store anything at the ferry ports, either. Most hotels and other accommodation types should be able to hold onto your luggage for you, but it is worth checking directly with the hotel at the time of booking. There are some independent services who will move your luggage around for you, such as Move My Bag (⊚ www. movemybag-isleofwight.co.uk), which can come in very handy if you are cycling or walking from point to point.

LGBTQ travellers
The Isle of Wight and England itself are generally tolerant places for the LGBTQ community. There's an annual LGBTQ Pride which takes place in Ryde (⊚ www.iwpride.org).

Lost property
Lost property (or anything found) should be reported on the Hampshire Police website here: ⊚ www.hampshire. police.uk/ro/report/lp/lost-or-found-property.

Maps
The Ordnance Survey (OS) produces the most comprehensive and detailed maps, renowned for their accuracy and clarity. Planning on going hiking or following simple trails? Then these are a must. Their 1:50,000 (pink) Landranger series shows enough detail to be useful for most walkers and cyclists, and there's more detail still in the full-colour 1:25,000 (orange) Explorer series. Both also have mobile versions available.

There's also a range of walking maps available in bookstores and online, and a selection at the *Medina* bookstore in West Cowes (see page 32).

If you only require a general route overview, however, there are various road atlases also available, at a scale of around 1:250,000.

Money (ATMs, banks, costs, credit cards, exchange)
Britain's currency is the pound sterling (£), divided into 100 pence (p). Coins come in denominations of 1p, 2p, 5p, 10p, 20p, 50p, £1 and £2. Notes are in denominations of £5, £10, £20 and £50. Scottish and Northern Irish banknotes are legal tender throughout Britain, though some traders may be unwilling to accept them. Some places accept euros. For current exchange rates, visit ⊚ xe.com.

Opening hours

Though traditional business hours are Monday to Saturday from around 9am to 5.30/6pm, most shops and supermarkets open earlier, close later and larger chains usually stay open on Sundays. Banks are closed at the weekends, but a few branches open on Saturday mornings. Smaller villages and more remote areas might have a tendency to do their own thing – but that's part of the charm.

Outside of the summer, a few places shut up shop for the off-season, but most of the major attractions stay open year-round (with the Christmas period a flexible exception).

Post offices

Pretty much every single post office is open Monday to Friday between 9am to 5.30pm, and until 1pm on Saturdays; some smaller branches are closed on Wednesday afternoons. Stamps can be bought here, but also from newsagents, many gift shops and supermarkets.

To find out your nearest post office, see ⓦ postoffice.co.uk.

Smoking

Smoking is banned in all public buildings and offices, restaurants and pubs, and on all public transport. Vaping – the use of e-cigarettes – is not allowed on public transport and is generally prohibited in museums and other public buildings; for restaurants and bars it depends on the individual proprietor and sometimes display a sign if permitted or not.

Time

Greenwich Mean Time (GMT) – equivalent to Coordinated Universal Time (UTC) – is used from the end of October to the end of March; for the rest of the year Britain switches to British Summer Time (BST), one hour ahead of GMT. GMT is five hours ahead of the US Eastern Standard Time and ten hours behind Australian Eastern Standard Time.

Tipping

Although there are no fixed rules for tipping, a ten to fifteen percent tip is anticipated by restaurant waiters. Some restaurants levy a "discretionary" or "optional" service charge of 10 or 12.5 percent. If they've done this, it should be clearly stated on the menu and on the bill. However, you are not obliged to pay the charge, and certainly not if the food or service wasn't what you expected. Cafés and bars may also leave a jar at the bar for small tips.

Toilets

There are public toilets available across the island, bus stations to wilder outposts; some are free, others incur a small charge.

Public holidays

Britain's public holidays (Bank Holidays), are:
January 1
Good Friday
Easter Monday
First Monday in May
Last Monday in May
Last Monday in August
December 25
December 26
Note that if January 1, December 25 or December 26 falls on a Saturday or Sunday, the next weekday becomes a public holiday.

Tourist information

There are 13 tourist information points on the Isle of Wight:

Bembridge
Brading
East Cowes
West Cowes
Freshwater Bay
Godshill
Havenstreet
Newport
Ryde
Sandown
Shanklin
Ventnor
Yarmouth

See Ⓦ www.visitisleofwight.co.uk/travel/tourist-information-points for details. Many places (hotels, museums, main bus stations) provide a selection of free brochures detailing different attractions around the island; hotel/B&B owners are usually happy to help; and some self-catering accommodation may provide information packs. The official island website, Ⓦ visitisleofwight.co.uk, has extensive coverage of the Isle of Wight, as does Ⓦ isleofwight.com.

Travellers with disabilities

There are plenty of disabled car parking spaces on the Isle of Wight, and buses accommodate wheelchairs and mobility scooters. The Island Line train service is also accessible.

All ferry and hovercraft options request 48hr notice before travelling if you are disabled; a blue badge is required by marine lawFor general planning tips and other useful resources, you can find out more on **Motability** (Ⓦ www.motability.co.uk).

Festivals and events

The iconic Isle of Wight Festival found its roots in 1968, but after the infamous 1970 festival, it was banned until 2002. The island is renowned for its sailing events, including the world-famous Cowes Week. There are plenty of carnivals, fayres and markets that promote the best the island has to offer locals and visitors of all ages. Here are some of the best, listed below.

Walk the Wight

May, Ⓦ isleofwightwalkingfestival.co.uk. The UK's longest-running and largest walking festival, including a cross-island trek for those who are up for something a bit extra. There are different walks to take that sees walkers covering sand dunes and quiet coves to bustling sailing towns and sleepy villages.

Isle of Wight Festival

June, Ⓦ isleofwightfestival.com. Annual festival that attracts major names, from Blondie and Jimi Hendrix to the Foo Fighters and Amy Winehouse. This is the biggest festival on the island and is one of the best-known across the entire country for its mix of music.

Round the Island Race

June/July, Ⓦ www.roundtheisland.org.uk. This is your chance to see some of the world's best sailors tackle the round-the-island race, which starts and finishes at Cowes. This one-day event attracts over 1400 boats and around 15,000 sailors, and there are numerous vantage points to get a good view.

Sandown Carnival

July, Ⓦ sandowncarnival.com. The Sandown Carnival has been running since 1889, filled with marching bands, lively parades, numerous events and fireworks at the island's south-coast resort.

The Wight Proms

July, Ⓦ www.wightproms.co.uk.

Held at Northwood Park in Cowes, the hugely popular Proms features comedy nights, classical performances, an outdoor cinema and free theatre workshops over the space of four days.

Cowes Week

Late July/early August,

🌐 aamcowesweek.co.uk.

One of the world's largest and much looked forward to sailing events, Cowes Week has been a key highlight in the British sporting calendar since it started in 1826. Olympic, world-class and weekend yachtsmen take part (in nearly 1000 boats) in different races over eight days.

Garlic Festival

August, 🌐 garlicfestival.co.uk.
This family-friendly festival offers live music, food stalls and a fun atmosphere. It's one of the largest and most popular events on the island.

Ventnor Fringe Festival

August, 🌐 vfringe.co.uk.
Make the most of the island's vibrant arts and culture centre at this six-day festival, including theatre, comedy, cabaret and musical performances.

Island Steam Show

August, 🌐 iwsteamrailway.co.uk.
Variety of displays and attractions, with comedy and entertainment arenas, live music, traditional fairground rides and working steam train demonstrations. There's also a range of vintage cars and old wagons, or hop on board for a classic steam train ride through the countryside.

International Charity Classic Car Show

September, 🌐 visitisleofwight.co.uk.
A fantastic range of vintage, classic, custom and retro cars descend to the island over a weekend, first parking at Newport Harbour before going on display in Ryde for visitors to have a look around.

Classic Buses, Beers and Walks Weekend

October, 🌐 iwbeerandbuses.co.uk.
Taking place over one weekend in October, classic and vintage buses from all over the UK (including the Bus Museum – see page 46) converge on the island and run a free, comprehensive network of routes – with many of the stops being real ale pubs. There are also footpath options for walkers.

Chronology

7000–6000 BC Isle of Wight forms as an island

43 AD Roman conquest of Britain, including Isle of Wight

280 Newport Roman Villa built

530 Saxons defeat Bowcombe Valley natives (near Newport) and takes island

686 Island is the last part of England to be converted to Christianity

1066 William Fitz Osbern is the first Lord of the island

1262 Isabella de Fortibus inherits Carisbrooke Castle

1362 English becomes the country's official language

1445 Henry Beauchamp crowned King of the Wight

1535 King Henry VIII instructs major fortification of island coastline

1545 Last French invasion

1582–84 Bubonic plague hits Newport

1584 Majority of pirates in the country are believed to be between Isle of Wight and Poole

1648 King Charles tries to escape from Carisbrooke Castle

1700 Bembridge Windmill built; Cowes shipbuilding yards established

1814 Ryde Pier opens

1827 The artist Turner paints while a guest at East Cowes Castle

1831 Twelve-year-old future Queen Victoria stays at Norris Castle

1833 Royal Yacht Squadron founded at Cowes

1843 Blackgang Chine opens

1838 Existing St Catherine's Lighthouse built

1845 Prince Regent Albert acquires Osborne House for his Queen Victoria

1849 Charles Dickens writes six chapters of *David Copperfield* at Winterbourne

1864 Julia Margaret Cameron takes first photographs at Dimbola Lodge

1901 Queen Victoria dies at Osborne House, aged 81

1942 Polish Destroyer ship *Blyskawica* defends Cowes in Second World War

1956–71 Secret rocket testing near Freshwater Bay

1968 First Isle of Wight Festival

1970 Legendary Isle of Wight Festival, where 600,000 hippies watch the likes of Jimi Hendrix, Joni Mitchell and The Who perform

1980 Isle of Wight International Scooter Rally launches

1995 Island restructures from two borough councils to one Isle of Wight Council

1999 First all-ladies crew row around the island, in 10 hours and 20 minutes

2002 The Isle of Wight Festival is reinstated

2004 Cowes Hammerhead Crane becomes Grade II listed

2019 Isle of Wight receives UNESCO Biosphere Reserve status

2020 BBC Countryfile Magazine Awards name Isle of Wight as Best Holiday Destination of the Year 2020

SMALL PRINT

Publishing Information
First edition 2020

Distribution
UK, Ireland and Europe
Apa Publications (UK) Ltd; sales@roughguides.com
United States and Canada
Ingram Publisher Services; ips@ingramcontent.com
Australia and New Zealand
Booktopia; retailer@booktopia.com.au
Worldwide
Apa Publications (UK) Ltd; sales@roughguides.com

Special Sales, Content Licensing and CoPublishing
Rough Guides can be purchased in bulk quantities at discounted prices. We can create special editions, personalised jackets and corporate imprints tailored to your needs. sales@roughguides.com.
roughguides.com

Printed in Poland

A catalogue record for this book is available from the British Library
The publishers and authors have done their best to ensure the accuracy and currency of all the information in **Pocket Rough Guide Isle of Wight**, however, they can accept no responsibility for any loss, injury, or inconvenience sustained by any traveller as a result of information or advice contained in the guide.

Rough Guide Credits
Editor: Carine Tracanelli
Head of Publishing: Sarah Clark
Cartography: Katie Bennett
Picture editor: Aude Vauconsant
Original design: Richard Czapnik

Senior DTP coordinator: Dan May
Head of DTP and Pre-Press: Rebeka Davies
Layout: Ruth Bradley

About the author
Aimee White is Senior Features Writer at LoveEXPLORING.com and a freelance travel writer. Prior to this, she was an Editor at Rough Guides and host of the *The Rough Guide to Everywhere* podcast. A Portsmouth girl born and raised, she has spent a lot of time sailing to and from the Isle of Wight. She has previously lived in China and the Czech Republic. Follow her on Twitter at @aimeefw.

Acknowledgements
Aimee would like to thank Sue Emerson at Visit Isle of Wight; Neil Chapman and Stephen Forster at Hovertravel; Katie and Maria Moore at Busingy House/Quay Management; and the teams at The Caledon, Jireh House, Royal Esplanade Hotel and North House, who probably took pity on a scruffy backpacker turning up at their lovely hotels!

Help us update
We've gone to a lot of effort to ensure that this edition of the **Pocket Rough Guide Isle of Wight** is accurate and up-to-date. However, things change – places get "discovered", opening hours are notoriously fickle, restaurants and rooms raise prices or lower standards. If you feel we've got it wrong or left something out, we'd like to know, and if you can remember the address, the price, the hours, the phone number, so much the better.

Please send your comments with the subject line "**Pocket Rough Guide Isle of Wight Update**" to mail@uk.roughguides.com. We'll credit all contributions and send a copy of the next edition (or any other Rough Guide if you prefer) for the very best emails.

Photo Credits
(Key: T-top; C-centre; B-bottom; L-left; R-right)

Alamy 12/13T, 14B, 16T, 26, 27, 34, 48, 71, 73, 88
Amanda Wheeler/The Crab Shed 72
Diana Jarvis/Rough Guides 33, 38
Eileen Long Photography/Inns of Distinction 55
English Heritage 23T
Getty Images 2T
iStock 2BC, 6, 12B, 14T, 15B, 15T, 17T, 18C, 19T, 20T, 47, 51, 56, 89
N.Cayla on Wikimedia Commons 59
Portsmouth City Council 96
Shutterstock 1, 2BL, 2C, 4, 5, 10, 11T, 11B, 13C, 18T, 19C, 20C, 20B, 21T, 21C, 22T, 22C, 22B, 23C, 29, 31, 35, 39, 42, 49, 60, 61, 62, 63, 66, 68, 70, 74, 82, 87, 90, 91, 92, 93, 94, 95, 97, 98, 99
Slab Artisan Fudge 32
User Nilfanion at Wikimedia Commons 23B
Vectis Ventures 41
www.visitisleofwight.co.uk 12/13B, 16B, 16/17B, 18B, 19B, 21B, 24/25, 37, 40, 43, 44, 52, 64, 65, 75, 77, 78, 80, 81, 83, 84, 86, 100/101, 108/109

Cover Shutterstock

Index